TEMPTATIONS OF RELIGION

TEMPTATIONS
OF RELIGION

Charles Davis

HARPER & ROW, PUBLISHERS

NEW YORK, EVANSTON, SAN FRANCISCO, LONDON

FOR CLAIRE

FIRST U.S. EDITION

Designed by Janice Stern

Library of Congress Cataloging in Publication Data

Davis, Charles, 1923–
   Temptations of religion.
   Includes bibliographical references.
   1. Religion. I. Title.
BL48.D3725   1974   200   73–6341
ISBN 0–06–061701–2

CONTENTS

I

THE LUST FOR CERTITUDE

A feature of the North American scene is the radio program given over to Gospel preachers of a fundamentalist kind. In listening occasionally to these programs when driving in the car, I feel repulsion, mixed with fascination. The overweening certitude has an almost physical effect upon me. The convictions are expressed fluently and skillfully, but with the onward rush of a one-track mind. The emotional strength of the certitude reveals the pressure of repressed doubt. That is not, I think, an unfair appraisal prompted by my disgust. The pressure beneath the certitude hisses out in a succession of condemnations of anything, from sexual permissiveness to evolutionary theory, which even remotely threatens the positions held.

But is not something of my reaction owing to the threat those people offer to my own position? Are not they the "true believers"? They would seem to have a much better claim to represent religion as found throughout history than those of a modern breed like myself, who combine certainty and uncertainty in a questioning faith.

Not all fundamentalists are like radio preachers—obnoxious. There is, I must admit, a strong case for claiming that all genuine religion requires absolute certitude.

First, has not religion traditionally offered certainty on all the important truths about man, the world and ultimate reality, and called for an unwavering acceptance? The standard portrait of the religious man presents him as living by great, simple, basic certainties, without losing his assurance in the face of trials and difficulties. The confidence of the religious man in the truths he holds has in every age been contrasted with the doubting or questioning attitude of the unbeliever or unconverted.

Again, according to most books of spiritual guidance for devout believers, doubts affecting faith are not to be entertained and weighed, but met by reaffirming faith in spite of them and by more fervent prayer and devotion.

Further, the common objection of linguistic philosophers against religious assertions as meaningful is that nothing is ever allowed to count against them; for example, no amount of evil and suffering in the world is allowed to overthrow the believer's conviction of God's love. Even if the objection is considered invalid, the possibility of making it shows unwavering certitude to be a recognized property of religious faith.

Lastly, the new religious movements, such as the Jesus People or the new Pentecostalists, proclaim a simple, unquestioning certitude. If they are anti-establishment, they are also antiliberal. Their adherents cannot abide the hesitations of those who live with a question mark above their religious beliefs and who are willing to revise those beliefs to meet new knowledge and fresh intellectual difficulties.

In brief, then, if I dislike the fundamentalist, is it not because he shows up my own inconsistency? Those like myself who do not yield themselves to a faith that excludes questions and doubts are, so it seems, trying to combine two incompatible attitudes, namely, reliance upon critical, autonomous reason and the obedient surrender of faith to a higher truth. The fundamentalist rejects the compromise.

I do not accept that conclusion. I think the fundamentalist has the matter wrong. All the same, he deserves a more detailed reply. I want to argue that the pursuit of certitude is not genuinely religious, but a temptation constantly besetting religious institutions and people. Indeed, the direct seeking of certitude corrupts religion and has the same relation to genuine faith as lust has to love. If we open ourselves to love, we overcome lust: if we open ourselves to faith, we overcome the obsession with certitude of the religious fundamentalist.

I want first to deal more concretely with the distortions produced in religion by an overconcern with certitude.

There are different types of religion. To ground their faith believers have appealed either to external authority or to inner experience. I should like to show how a whoring after certitude has damaged each of these forms of religious faith.

An appeal to a visible, external authority, such as the Church or the Bible, as grounding faith is in effect the acceptance of a system of symbolic mediation. This is because religious faith as ultimate concern must always be taken as in the last analysis resting upon God himself or the Ultimate. The external authority, therefore, has to be understood as a symbol mediating the higher, divine authority. Different forms of external authority represent different systems of symbolic mediation. There have been a number of these in the course of religious history.

In Christian history the most elaborate system to be found is the hierarchical, sacramental order of medieval Christendom. Faith was originated and sustained through the ritual, creeds, laws, and institutions of a comprehensive system of spiritual mediation. This was seen as built into the structure of the cosmos and affecting its functioning. As well as the Church on earth it included a heavenly hierarchy of saints and angels with their merits and prayers.

When the medieval system was functioning healthily, the certitude of faith was not the object of any particular concern or striving. Certitude was there, but as an assurance consequent upon a life within the stable order of spiritual mediation, not as something sought for directly and made a special gift or achievement. Theology reflected that outlook. In his great work, the *Summa Theologiae*, Thomas Aquinas, unlike later theological writers, did not set out to prove theses, determining for each its degree of certitude in relation to the faith. Instead, he pursued the understanding of faith through a wide variety of questions, without trying to measure the certitude of all his answers.

The famines and the Black Death that ravaged Europe in the fourteenth century caused a breakdown in the functioning of the established symbolic order. Under the pressure of the situation, the system of spiritual mediation was no longer sufficiently able to counteract the destructive impact of death upon society and upon the meaning embodied in the social order. From that time on many sought for their spiritual remedy outside the established system. The old symbolic order came under attack. Since then it has had to defend itself against the disruptive movements of the fourteenth and fifteenth centuries, against the Reformation, the Enlightenment and the collapse in the French

Revolution of the system of political authority that had served as its counterpart.

So, in the Roman Catholic Church we find the medieval symbolic order, much battered by history, still trying to survive in the secular world of today.

Understandably, if in my opinion still wrongly, the protectors of the threatened order tried to quell their own doubts and repel the skeptical attacks of dissenters by directly bolstering certitude. The first treatises on the Church appeared in the fourteenth century, containing what Yves Congar has dubbed a hierarchology.[1] From then onward came an ever increasing insistence upon the authority of the visible Church and the papacy. Against Protestantism and on the basis of the decrees of the Council of Trent was created the closed order and tight discipline of a diminished Catholic Church. Opposition to the rising secular movements of the modern world, with their questioning of traditional beliefs and norms, led to a further stress on the authority of the Church, meaning the hierarchy, in matters of faith and morals. The eventual definition of papal infallibility as a dogma by the First Vatican Council in the nineteenth century was a defiant proclamation of the unfailing authority and efficacy of the old order of mediation, issued to comfort the faithful and confound unbelievers in the disintegration consequent upon the French Revolution.

The definition of papal infallibility is the culminating point in the attempts of the old order of Christendom to use direct appeals to authority as means to secure religious certitude against new questioning and doubts. Some comments, then, on what may be called the papal solution to modern doubt will illustrate my general thesis.

The question of the pope's infallibility has now entered a new phase in Catholic theology. This began with the open denial of the defined doctrine by the theologian Hans Küng in his book, *Infallible? An Inquiry.*[2] Polemically and ecclesiastically, the book was important, but it was imperfect on the scholarly level. Its defects of scholarship, however, were more than made up for by a book published two years later by the outstanding medievalist Brian Tierney.[3]

The latter finds the origins of the idea of papal infallibility in the fierce disputes over the Franciscan doctrine of poverty at the end of the thirteenth and the beginning of the fourteenth centuries. Paradoxically, the doctrine that later was to represent the supreme exaltation of the papacy began as an attempt to limit the sovereignty of the pope by making papal decrees irrevocable and thus preventing any future pope from going back upon the declarations of his predecessors.

The use of the idea of irrevocability to limit papal power was first devised by the eccentric theologian Pietro Olivi at the end of 1279. In August of that year, Pope Nicholas III had issued the bull *Exiit,* strongly supporting the Franciscan doctrine of poverty. Olivi wanted to exclude the possibility of any change on the part of a future pope. Although he did not use the word "infallible," he did, as Tierney argues, introduce the idea of the irreformability and inerrancy of papal judgments.

In fact, in 1323 a pope, John XXII, reversed the teaching of his predecessor on poverty, a matter he regarded as a question of discipline not of faith. Uproar followed. We need not bother with the polemics, but one item is worth noting. In the debate Guido Terreni wrote in support of the Pope, but managed with the aid of distinctions to affirm papal infallibility, using the word itself. He thus became the first theoretician of the doctrine.

In the light of his historical investigation, Tierney contends that the doctrine of papal infallibility did not arise by the gradual unfolding of a truth always held in the Church. It came in as a novelty in the context of the polemics over the Franciscan doctrine of poverty. Previous to that, there had been a settled agreement among the canonists that the pope could err, though divine providence would prevent the whole Church from being led astray. As a matter of fact, the novel teaching did not find much favor and remained dormant, until, with its historical origins forgotten, the idea proved advantageous in the sixteenth and seventeenth centuries against Protestants and Gallicans.

For our present purpose the main bearing of Tierney's book does not lie in his reconstruction of the historical circumstances in which the idea of papal infallibility first explicitly arose, brilliant though that is. It lies in the conviction the book has generated that historical criticism has finally undermined the dogma. Papal infallibility, it would now seem clear, does not represent an organic development of previous Christian teaching, but a novelty introduced for ulterior motives and subsequently exploited for controversial purposes. But at this point I wonder whether the Tierney approach is enough.

To explain. I am no defender of papal infallibility. I consider it well established by modern scholarship that there is no sufficient basis for the papal claim either in Scripture or in the first centuries of Christian tradition. In brief, if we disregard, as we must, Catholic arguments as special pleading, papal infallibility has been an intellectually negligible thesis for some time. For that reason, studies such as Tierney's are welcome as helping us to trace the beginnings and early history of an upstart idea emerging late in the Christian tradition. But once the business of either establishing or refuting the doctrine is left aside as belonging to the past, the task that should now loom large for the student of religion is a better understanding of the way "the infallible pope" functioned as a religious symbol.

Undoubtedly the papacy acquired a symbolic force in the Catholic religion. To say this in no way denies the political factors in the development of papal power nor the contingent circumstances, such as the controversies with the Franciscan Spirituals, affecting the formulation of its claims. But it does mean that the papacy came to embody as a symbol—however inadequately and with distortions—many elements of the Christian religious heritage. That is why Congar in his review of the book[4] can maintain that Tierney's account—valid as it might be within limits—does not account for all the content of the doctrine of papal infallibility as it later developed. For example, it became the visible symbol of the unity of the Church and the indefectibility of its faith. Where Congar and others claim too much is in supposing that because the doctrine through contingent historical circumstances became a vehicle of authentically Christian themes it has a permanent place and ground in the Christian tradition.

What, then, is most needed is not an account of the content or history of the doctrine. The present need is for studies in religious typology, relating the structures of papal sovereignty at different times with forms of religious consciousness and likewise official papal ideologies with popular religious symbols and convictions. To draw a comparison. We no longer debate the truth or falsity of the divine right of kings, but we do study it seriously as a form of political consciousness. Similarly, the papal claim is no longer a question for intellectual debate, but we need to analyze its functioning within the religious consciousness of Catholics.

If we approach papal infallibility from that point of view, then unquestionably its function when it was defined in 1870 was to provide a bulwark of religious certitude against attacks on the Church from all sides in the general breakup of the traditional order of Christendom. It came out of the same defensive mentality that produced the Syllabus of Errors of 1865, rejecting all that the modern world stood for. Those were the days when William George Ward, the Oxford convert, wanted a papal bull with his breakfast every morning. The definition of 1870 did not take the extreme form Ward desired. All the same, his mentality illustrates well why the idea of papal infallibility became prominent in the nineteenth century and what insistence upon it was intended to achieve. The great preoccupation of Ward as a religious thinker was with religious certitude. He looked to the authority of the papacy to secure the certitude of Christian faith against modern doubt.

Here I return to my general point: religious certitude cannot be directly sought or secured. The appeal to infallibility no longer works. In issuing *Humanae Vitae,* the encyclical of 1968 condemning contraception, the pope did not invoke infallibility, but that encyclical marks the end of papal authority as a source of religious certitude for Catholics. With hindsight we can now see that an attempt to bolster certitude by declaring an infallible authority was doomed to failure. To confirm this with a brief analysis:

The claim to infallibility may be taken on two different levels: as a doctrine and as a symbol.

As a doctrine the claim as defined is a very limited affirmation in which the conditions of an infallible utterance are strictly determined. But the doctrine thus limited has proved of little use, whether theoretical or practical. As a theoretical principle it has not helped in interpreting and evaluating data from the history of papal teaching, because one can always argue in regard to any past doctrine that the precise conditions for an infallible statement were not fulfilled. As a practical norm for present teaching, it has remained largely in abeyance, because, as someone humorously remarked, an infallible pope cannot afford to make a mistake. The only clear instances of the fulfillment of the conditions, one instance before and one after the definition of 1870, are the dogmas of the Immaculate Conception and of the Assumption of Mary, doctrines asserted gratuitously and without any data in the New Testament and early tradition against which they can be checked.

Infallibility has always functioned chiefly as a symbol. Many have noticed how the claim to infallibility has spread an aura of unquestionable certitude over teaching with no infallible guarantee. It misses the mark to refer contemptuously to this phenomenon as "creeping infallibility." That is to view infallibility from a narrowly intellectual standpoint as functioning merely as a doctrinal formulation. But in its social and historical context, the claim to infallibility was intended as an assurance that the Roman Catholic Church, governed and taught by the pope, remains a trustworthy guide in matters of faith and morals. The pope as infallible was a symbol, focusing and strengthening the reliance of the faithful upon the mediation of the hierarchical Church in all that concerned their salvation. It always was an essential part of its symbolic function to impart a sense of certitude in regard to all Church teaching, not just in regard to *ex cathedra* definitions.

The infallible pope as symbol worked as long as the Roman Catholic system as a whole remained unquestioned from within. The symbol functioned as a rallying cry for besieged Catholics. But now that the traditional order based upon the papacy has come under serious question by Catholics themselves and the boundaries dividing them from others are no longer clearly drawn, infallibility has quickly proved to be an empty symbol.

Of its nature the system of papal infallibility is an act of violence to the religious consciousness, an attempt to force certitude as a necessary result of compliance with a set of external, juridical norms. If, so the system supposes, the pope fulfills a set of juridical conditions, his declarations are true with absolute certainty; if a Catholic conforms to that papal teaching, he can be absolutely certain that his beliefs are true. The certitude is secured by fulfilling a set of legal conditions. However, the process simply transfers the problem of certitude from the content of faith to the validity of the claims of external authority, so that the move becomes quite useless once those claims are no longer taken for granted but called seriously into question. Moreover, the shift from reliance upon faith itself in its content to external authority cuts the believer off from the only source of genuine religious certitude.

In saying this, I am not objecting to forms of religious faith, such as Catholic Christianity, which appeal to external institutions as mediating religious experience. But where there is an order of symbolic mediation, genuine religious certitude does not come from the mediating institutions in themselves but from what they mediate. Once a system of mediation turns in upon itself and tries to establish confidence on the ground of the indefectibility or infallibility of its institutions and procedures, it becomes opaque and ceases to mediate. It then engages in circular, frustrating efforts to defend its authority by its authority and to ground its certitude upon its certitude about itself. A mediating institution gains credence for itself by effectively mediating. In brief, for the papacy to regain its authority, Christians must experience the papacy as an effective mediator of Christian truth and life. But if they did so, there would be no need for the symbol of infallibility. The mediating Church could then be constructed as a symbol in a fashion more in accord with man's consciousness of his freedom and individual responsibility.

The form of religious consciousness represented by papal infallibility might be described as institutional fundamentalism. However, the term "fundamentalism" usually refers to a similar development in a different religious system. Let us turn, then, to other religious systems within Christianity.

The collapse of the medieval system led Luther at the Reformation to reject the mediation of faith by external authority and to ground faith, which he interpreted as trust, upon an inwardly experienced assurance of being personally justified through Christ. His appeal was essentially to inner experience, but he kept some external elements from the old symbolic order. The stress upon the Bible and preaching in Luther and the other Reformers led subsequently in Protestantism to the development of a new system of symbolic mediation, in which the external authority was the Bible. According to this religious system, faith was originated and sustained by the Word of God as found in the Bible. God spoke to men in the words of the Bible. The life of the Church and the life of the individual Christian were centered upon the preaching and hearing of the biblical Word of God.

Because of the endless polemics resulting from the Reformation, this religion of the Word could not function as unselfconsciously as the medieval system in its heyday. The word "Protestant" implies an act of protest, and Protestantism began as a protest against the medieval Church. With all the rich positive content of the Protestant faith, the negative awareness that there were those who did not abide by the true Word of God was always present. This negative element prevented the Protestant world from acquiring the taken-for-granted character of the medieval order. The gain-sayers of God's Word were in the first place the Catholics or papists, against whose abuses the Reformers had taken their stand. But soon Protestants themselves were divided over the interpretation of the Word. In particular, there was the tension between the major Protestant churches and the dissenting, radical groups. These latter saw themselves as the only true followers of God's biblical Word.

Perhaps I can illustrate the role of the negative in Protestant self-understanding by two examples, both from England. Foxe's *Book of Martyrs,* recounting the persecution of the Protestants under the Catholic queen, Mary Tudor, was almost a second Bible in the England of the late sixteenth and seventeenth centuries. It burned an anti-Catholic consciousness deep into the English soul. Then there is the spiritual classic, *The Pilgrim's Progress,* written by the dissenter John Bunyan. An immensely popular book, it represents biblical Christianity at its best. But, though subdued, the polemical element is there, and we remember that the author had spent twelve years in Bedford jail for his preaching.

My purpose is not to underplay the positive witness of Protestant Christianity. I simply wish to point out that the certitude of its religious convictions included a negative stance against other positions as a prominent and essential ingredient. For that reason it opened the way for further negative questioning.

Nevertheless, for a period the Protestant system in its various groupings did mediate Christian truth to people as an assured basis for their lives without any forced effort to build an impregnable certitude immediately upon its own authority. It operated smoothly upon the unquestioned assumption that the Bible was the very Word of God.

The decisive attack upon the system came with the modern critical study of the Bible. From the nineteenth century onward biblical Christianity as a religious system has been continuously threatened. In many groups this has turned the system in upon itself, in an attempt to bolster certitude and repress doubts by a rigid insistence upon the authority of the Bible as literally interpreted. Hence the biblical fundamentalism already mentioned.

Tillich makes a useful distinction between two stages of literalism, the natural and the reactive.[5]

The natural stage of literalism precedes the making of a clear distinction between the symbolic and the factual; in Tillich's words, it consists "in the inability to separate the creations of symbolic imagination from the facts which can be verified through observation and experiment." Such literalism is merely the naïveté inevitable before growth in consciousness and the differentiation of meanings growth brings.

Very different is that reactive literalism which insists upon a literal interpretation after "the breaking of the myth," that is, after the symbolic character of religious language has been discerned. Literalism in the second stage is "aware of the questions but re-presses them, half consciously, half unconsciously." It is chosen by "people who prefer the repression of their questions to the uncertainty which appears with the breaking of the myth."

Perhaps the word "literalism" is inappropriate for the primitive stage of consciousness, because the symbolic was there, though fused with the literal in that stage. The valid point made by Tillich may be expressed more accurately by drawing upon the reflections of Owen Barfield[6] on the history of language. Barfield argues, convincingly I think, that both the literal and the consciously metaphorical are derivative senses, coming later in the evolution of consciousness and language. The common opinion that words originally had merely a plain literal sense, referring to physical objects and events, and then that sense was extended by conscious metaphor to invisible and spiritual realities is an assumption un-supported by the data and due to philosophical prejudice. The first stage of language Barfield calls figurative. At this stage what later became the literal and metaphorical levels of meaning were still undifferentiated. For example, the word "heart" did not at first mean solely the physical organ and was then applied by a conscious metaphor to spiritual and psychological realities. The literal sense, as used in the science of anatomy, of a mere physical object, stripped of any spiritual dimension, is a late development, requiring a high degree of differentiation in consciousness. "Heart" began as having a figurative meaning that included both physical and spiritual levels of reference without distinguishing them.

From this standpoint, reactive literalism, Tillich's second stage, is an attempt to cramp the figurative language of the Bible into the narrow framework of interpretation appropriate only to the literal usage of modern science. Admittedly, the language of empirical science has had a considerable impact upon ordinary language, so that much modern speech is denuded of any but empirical meaning and shares the literalness of scientific language. That is why the modern Bible reader is tempted to take a literal or factual interpretation as basic and normative for every text, except the obviously poetic. But this is to distort the meaning of the Bible by reading it in anachronistic manner. To give a crude instance: the attempt, known as concordism, to reconcile the creation account with modern science by interpreting the six days as geological periods. The tables of correspondences ingeniously worked out did not gain the respect of scientists and, what was worse, exchanged the religious meaning of the biblical narrative for a pottage of pseudo-facts.

The distortions, however, have not all been on the part of believers. The critical study of the Bible was marked, especially in its early stages, by a rationalism as blind as fundamentalism to the nature of the religious language of the Bible. Too easily the factual inaccuracy of the biblical record has been taken as destroying its religious meaning. The critics often manifested the same intolerance of ambiguity, the same desire for immediate clarity and certitude, as their conservative opponents.

Undoubtedly, the controversies about the truth of the Bible have shown how widespread among believers is the lust for certitude. The ramifications of the critical study of the Bible are too many to outline here. However, its effects can be summed up by saying that modern criticism has introduced a far-reaching uncertainty into the authority and meaning of the Bible. It has raised so many questions that it has made impossible a simple, straightforward use of the Bible as the very Word of God.

Biblical fundamentalism is a refusal to live with the uncertainty thus created by modern thought. It reacts by a narrow literalism of interpretation and a wooden insistence upon the verbal inerrancy of the Bible.

Here again a system of symbolic mediation—the Bible as God's Word—has become opaque by aiming directly at certitude. It does achieve a kind of certitude, but by repression rather than by mediating a truth unafraid of itself.

Luther's religion of inner experience, apart from its retention of elements from medieval sacramentalism, remained within the setting of a traditional social and political order. That order functioned as a system of temporal mediation, conveying attitudes, values, and modes of authority and submission. In the Middle Ages it had formed a unity with the sacramental, hierarchical order of the Church. Luther, though he attacked the medieval system of spiritual mediation, feared the collapse of the temporal system, and, indeed, invoked its support for his reforms.

For a stark appeal to inner experience outside any established system of mediation we have to turn to the nineteenth century and to Kierkegaard, whose influence, if delayed, has been profound upon modern Protestant thought.

Faith for Kierkegaard is passionate inwardness with objective uncertainty. To explain this . . .

Truth is subjectivity, Kierkegaard declared. He did not mean, as some have thought, that all knowledge rested upon merely subjective criteria.[7] Though less quoted, the more frequent form of his statement is, Subjectivity is truth. The concern of Kierkegaard in the context was not with the conditions of knowledge, but with what it means to exist as a human being. He was arguing that man is in a state of truth as a human being, that is truly human, when he is fully subjective. To exist in truth as a human being is not a matter of knowing objectively what a human being is, but of actualizing that truth inwardly. Kierkegaard was reacting against the stress in Hegel upon objectivity and universality. The way to enter into a state of truth as a human being, Kierkegaard contended, is not by rational, impersonal, universal knowledge, but by inwardness and personal commitment, by becoming subjective not objective.

He applies this to the relationship with God, who is eternal truth. A human being does not achieve unity with God through becoming objective and rational, but by a leap of faith, which is nonrational. Faith is nonrational because its commitment is without objective certainty. But the passion required for that commitment realizes subjectivity. Faith, to repeat, is passionate inwardness with objective uncertainty.

We can see now why Kierkegaard insists so much upon the Incarnation as the supreme paradox. For him the Christian paradox, namely that God became man, is not just uncertain objectively, but absurd for objective reason. But for that very reason it intensifies subjectivity. To achieve the passion necessary to make a leap of faith affirming that supreme paradox is to reach the greatest intensification of one's inwardness. It is thus to attain full subjectivity, which is truth. Truth for the Christian believer does not reside in objectivity.

Kierkegaard has much of value to say about what it means to

be a human being and also about the subjective attitude necessary for the attainment of religious truth. To suppose that entry into religious faith is a matter of impersonal, objective reason or that religious truth is available to any detached inquirer is a mistake made by rationalists and empiricists. However, Kierkegaard's insights in this respect were distorted, it seems to me, by indefensible attempts to offer a passionate inwardness of appropriation as proof or, apparently at times, even replacement for the objective content of faith.[8] That content he generally held to, but, despite his protest against objectivity, it does ineluctably demand objective grounding. The paradoxical character of the Incarnation, with the consequent intensification of the passion required for faith, does not justify our affirming it.

The reason for Kierkegaard's exaggerated repudiation of objectivity lies, I suggest (though it would take too long to prove it here), in an excessive concern with certitude and his direct pursuit of it. He acknowledged the objective uncertainty confronting the Christian believer, but he wanted to avoid the subjective consequences of that. He felt he had to go after nothing less than complete certitude of inward conviction, in order to participate in Christianity and in the eternal happiness it promised. Kierkegaard could not relinquish the absolute certitude he associated with Christian faith, and in a *tour de force* he made the objective uncertainty bolster the subjective certitude by his concept of paradox.

Much modern Protestant thought, especially the neo-orthodox variety, has sought an unassailable certitude of faith by appealing to subjectivity and refusing objective reason a role. But the history of that approach would seem to show that no stable solution will in that way be found to the problems raised by faith. Faith is not the product of reason, but to exclude reason from faith is to thrust faith outside much of human living. Faith thus set apart in pure subjectivity loses its hold upon men. It is in that way that the pursuit of certitude has often led to the destruction of faith.

I have been examining different types of Christian religions: the medieval hierarchical order, prolonged especially in Roman Catholicism but also to some extent in Protestantism; the appeal to the Bible alone as the Word of God; and the reliance upon inner experience. I have tried to show how each of these systems of faith has suffered distortions by an excessive concern with certitude. The hierarchical Church with the collapse of Christendom has tried to support itself by itself, by proclaiming itself infallible; in reaction against modern criticism the fundamentalist has turned the Bible into an inerrant oracle, crudely interpreted as a literal, factual record; inward conviction faced with uncertainty has been used to justify the exclusion of objective reason. The conclusion I have been working toward is that in religion direct attempts to achieve certitude are self-defeating. Each system of faith has in effect become closed in upon itself by the efforts to keep its adherents in absolute certitude. Such self-enclosure violates the nature of religious faith, which implies a self-transcending openness to total reality.

But the reader is entitled to ask for some more constructive comments. Can one live a life of faith with questioning and doubts? What does it mean to believe today without retreating into the confines of some supposedly self-justifying system? Let me try to explain how I personally see the matter.

I think the believer today must first recognize how far the certainties of our ordinary, everyday existence are due to social conformity. What we take for granted as reality is in fact a social construction. I am drawing here upon the writings of Peter Berger and his collaborator, Thomas Luckmann.[9] I find their sociological analysis of knowledge convincing. It shows us how far our knowledge and indeed our inner life as a whole are socially conditioned. Some brief general remarks will provide a background for what I want to say about faith.

The relation between the individual and society is dialectical. Society is the product of men, and men are the product of society. These are not contradictory statements, but the expression of a dialectic, namely of the mutual interaction of two opposed but linked principles of change.

Society is a human product. The socio-cultural world in its entirety is the creation of human activity and is kept in existence only by the continuance of human activity. When the pattern of human activity underlying any social institution changes or ceases, that institution changes or ceases. Men create and sustain the world in which they live. They do so both by changing their physical environment by bodily activity and by pouring human meaning into external forms, such as language, myths, rites, family, tribe, and state. Social institutions, such as parliaments, law courts, and universities, essentially consist in externalized human meaning.

The distinctively human or socio-cultural world, which is the ordered environment in which men live their lives, is a social construction. It is created and maintained by men together in their social activity.

But men are the product of society. The individual comes to be as a person only in and through the action of the social environment upon him. From infancy onward by socialization he internalizes the social reality that surrounds him. That social reality is drawn into his consciousness and is built into him as the structure of his inner life. His thought and imagination, his emotions and activity are ordered into a pattern given by the culture in which he has been formed, and he depends upon society for the continuance of his attitudes and activity, which otherwise would disintegrate and become meaningless. Through and through men are social beings; society is not just a useful arrangement external to them. Take language as an example. It is socially created and socially maintained in its changing development. Yet consider how the language an individual receives from his culture, patterns his thought and his emotions.

Nevertheless, we must not forget that the relation between society and the individual is dialectical. The individual is not molded by society as a passive, inert thing. He interacts with society during socialization, so that the existing social reality is modified during transmission from one generation to the next, and on reaching maturity the person becomes an active participant in the social process, able consciously to work for social change.

Further, we should distinguish between what is made available by society and what is dominant within it. As societies become more complex and, furthermore, stand at the end of a long tradition of civilization they include many elements in their cultural heritage that conflict with the attitudes and spirit now dominant in the society. Social deviants may have rich resources made available to them socially to help them stand apart from the present spirit of their society. But the limits and conditions of the refusal to conform to contemporary society should be recognized.

What most men take as real is what is accepted and confirmed by society as a whole. The reality of the everyday world in which men live has a taken-for-granted quality, which comes to it from being socially shared and socially confirmed. Social institutions and social activities constantly presuppose and reinforce what society understands as real; this "knowledge" and this "reality" are difficult to question and by most are unquestioned. Whatever lies outside this socially shared and socially confirmed knowledge does not have the same accent of reality. It seems to lack solidity and does not impose itself with the same matter-of-fact clarity upon the mind. What is confirmed generally by society conveys a sense of unmistakable reality; what is held only as a private opinion has the feel of a fugitive and tenuous reality.

All our knowledge has a social dimension; it is dependent upon social experience. The social basis underlying our knowledge may be called its plausibility structure, because it is in social sharing that our opinions receive that confirmation which makes them plausible. The opinions dominant in a particular culture are supported by a massive plausibility structure, which gives what they affirm a taken-for-granted reality. Deviant opinions have a weak plausibility structure, which means that the reality of what they affirm is constantly challenged and threatened even within the consciousness of those who hold them. The position of a cognitive minority is not easy, either socially or psychologically.

At the same time, we must not confuse the question of truth and validity with the question of what is accepted or not by a particular society. The sociological investigation of what is "knowledge" or "reality" for a society brackets the philosophical questions concerning truth and reality. Astrology was part of reality as taken for granted by ancient Babylonian society; that does not make it true in more than a limited social sense. What astronomy affirms is socially confirmed reality for us, but that reason alone does not give it more than a relative validity. Most of what is affirmed by modern science is not part of the world as socially shared and confirmed as real by the Australian aborigines; that does not make it false.

We have indeed to face the fact that all our knowledge is socially conditioned, but that need not lead us into complete relativism. As Peter Berger himself remarks:

> When everything has been subsumed under the relativizing categories in question (those of history, of the sociology of knowledge, or what-have-you), the question of truth reasserts itself in almost pristine simplicity. Once we know that all human affirmations are subject to scientifically graspable socio-historical processes, *which affirmations are true and which are false?* We cannot avoid the question any more than we can return to the innocence of its pre-relativizing asking.[10]

Or, let me put it in my own way. Total relativism is incoherent because it maintains as a universal standpoint that there is no universal standpoint. Nor is there cause to relapse into a despairing indifference to any pursuit of knowledge and value beyond the changing fictions of society. Although it is impossible to separate the universal from the relative in our truths and values, there is a discernible universality. It may be discerned in the general possibility of communication, in the constant recurrence of the same questions, in the easy agreement concerning the greatness of certain thinkers and writings, in the overlapping and convergence of ideas and norms. Further, the dependence of all our thinking upon the social process and social conditions does not make the question of its truth or falsity nugatory, any more than the similar dependence of the whole of our thinking upon the brain does so. The question of truth or falsity concerns the content or essential nature of our thoughts, not the material and social substructure upon which they depend for their origin and continuance.

What, however, is excluded, it seems to me, is a revelation insofar as that implies an a priori claim to absoluteness and universality. Revelation in that sense is given as an absolute in the order of knowledge; it is regarded as a set of unquestionable data, from which all opinions may be evaluated. It represents an attempt to limit criticism, to put a stop to the endless questioning of human thinking by establishing an a-critical point, a point not subject to criticism because beyond criticism.[11] To reject revelation in that sense is not to exclude a guiding and inspiring intervention of God, a manifestation of God in word and event, the Word of God as embodied in the words of men. But it is to exclude an a priori absoluteness and universality as violating human intelligence and freedom. No body of religious truths and values, emerging as these must in a particular society and culture, can be more than potentially universal. Any universality present with them has to be gradually actualized as the truths and values are taken up into other cultures. At the same time, the transcultural process will point up the relativity of many of the elements. Further, within the culture in which the religion emerged, there will be the unending effort to question existing truths, an effort constitutive of human intelligence. It is a misconception of faith to suppose that it can shortcut either the reflection of centuries or the transcultural process and make a priori a claim to absoluteness and universality. It can no more do that than answer a historical question without historical evidence. To interpret "revelation" in that way is to take a mythical image as describing a literal fact. If the relativity that marks all human knowledge does not mean that all our truths and values are social fictions and does not exclude the human thrust toward truth as absolute and universal, it does exclude absolute and universal truth as being served up on a plate under the heading of divine revelation. The awareness of the extent to which our "knowledge" is a social construction with no further validity than confirmation by present society and of the slow, dialectical process and criticism of social fictions by which men must move toward truth and value destroys the easy certitude of the religious fundamentalist. The awakening to social mythology is indeed particularly sharp for religious people, because of religion's shift of place in modern society.

No form of religious faith receives today the massive social confirmation required to make its content part of taken-for-granted reality. Whatever may be the difference of opinion among sociologists about the nature and degree of secularization, the Christian religion has clearly lost its monopoly, and no other form of faith has taken its place as the exclusive world-view of Western society. It is possible to live and be effectually operative in present society with any of a number of religious or para-religious convictions or with none. In that sense religion is no longer social fact. It does not confront men as part of that objective world the reality of which is created and constantly confirmed day after day by social institutions, social activities, and social opinion. It has the lesser reality that belongs to matters of private opinion and personal preference.

This situation has a twofold effect upon the believer: spiritual and emotional.

Spiritually, the believer has to come to terms with the uncomfortable fact that the world of faith no longer has that accent of reality which is given by the confirmation and approval of society as a whole. In our culture faith and all that faith talks about are surrounded by an air of unreality. There is that much truth in the assertion that God is dead. It was not so in a Christian culture. The world of faith was part of that taken-for-granted reality which was supported at every turn by society and its activities.

Faith today has therefore shifted its place in our consciousness. Where it is more than nominal, it has become more a function of personal conviction and decision than it was before. Certainly, as any personal conviction, faith still needs some social support, so that the believer must seek the company of others in a community of believers. But unless that community closes itself off as a sect from the wider society, it will never achieve the unity of faith among its members such as was achieved in the past by the massive confirmation of society.

The second effect of his situation in modern culture upon the believer is emotional. Believers do not and cannot feel their faith in the same way as they did in a confident Christian culture. That is why so much devotional and liturgical expression strikes the struggling believer today as emotionally untrue. People, I think, are often trying to express this when they say that such-and-such prayers or rites are meaningless. Unacceptable doctrinal implications can be neutralized by taking them historically as past interpretations of the Christian faith. The emotional tone is more likely to cause trouble. Its impact cannot be easily neutralized. Consequently, insensitive efforts to resuscitate the devotional attitudes of the past create an unbearable sense of pretense and insincerity.

On the other hand, an immense religious advantage is to be gained from the cessation of Christianity as social myth. Religion as the quest for the ultimate should rightly have the effect of making men see through the forms of their society, of shattering social myths and exposing the relativity of all human institutions and conceptual systems. This function, however, often becomes forgotten through the dominance of the other function of religion, namely, the support of society through providing a comprehensive system of meaning within which the social order can be built. But when this second function is exercised without reference to the first, religion falls into the idolatry of making a relative social order and a relative structure of meanings absolute or sacred in itself. Now that the Christian faith is no longer the dominant myth of Western society, it may stand forth in its starkness for the believer as a quest for the transcendent beyond all cultural forms, including those of Western Christendom.

From that standpoint I think that Christians today have been ill served by radical or secular theologians. These have too easily accepted the reality presuppositions of modern society and accommodated the Christian message to those presuppositions, without recognizing the relativity of modern consciousness. When they say, as in so many words they often do, "We cannot today accept such-and-such," the question to be asked is: "Do you mean that such-and-such is excluded by a critical examination based on appropriate criteria of truth and falsity, or do you mean that we cannot get such-and-such across to people today because it is out of accord with their socially confirmed convictions?" If the latter is the case, the appropriate response is, "So what?" The socially confirmed world of modern society is as relative as any other socio-cultural world. It cannot be accepted as a norm unless one wishes to be imprisoned in social myth. If I may quote Peter Berger again:

> The theologian is consequently deprived of the psychologically liberating possibility of either radical commitment or radical negation. What he is left with, I think, is the necessity for a step-by-step re-evaluation of the traditional affirmations in terms of his own cognitive criteria (which need *not* necessarily be those of a putative "modern consciousness"). Is this or that in the tradition true? Or is it false? I don't think that there are shortcut answers to such questions, neither by means of "leaps of faith" nor by the methods of any secular discipline.[12]

In brief, "modern" and "out of date" are not equivalent to "true" and "false"—or at least they are only for those who are still the prey of social fictions.

To suffer the awakening of consciousness that brings recognition of the social construction of our reality, with the extent to which our "knowledge" and "values" are social fictions and the relativity marking our deepest thoughts and ideals, is to look into the abyss, the void, surrounding human life in every direction. We can respond to the nothingness by a nihilism that interprets it as chaos, as meaninglessness, as the ultimate absurdity making everything absurd. Or we can respond to the void as positive nothingness, as mystery. That is the religious response. Faith in the last analysis is a basic trust in reality, an openness to mystery, a being drawn toward the abyss in self-forgetfulness and awe and love. Faith acknowledges the relativities of finite human existence without the nihilistic denial that these do, however gropingly, lead us toward absolute meaning and value.

All that is very different from the claim that religion provides us with a set of absolute certainties concerning God, man, and the universe. But an insistence upon absolute certitude misconceives religion, even from a narrowly intellectual standpoint. Intellectually, religion is a search for meaning rather than certitude.

Even the scientific enterprise, dependent as it is upon empirical verification, would come to a halt if scientists insisted upon nothing less than certitude before proceeding further. Scientific knowledge would include little if limited to certainties; it is made up of probabilities, approximations, and hypotheses. The scientist himself is seeking to understand rather than to be certain. His assurance that he is on the right track arises from his growing understanding of the data.

Religious thought, too, flourishes, not when theologians are carefully weighing degrees of certitude and religious authorities are insisting upon infallibility or inerrancy, but when the religious community is actively concerned with understanding its faith in relation to the concrete data of its experience, both individual and social.

Besides, the objective content of faith is embodied in the first place, not in propositions, to which degrees of certainty can be attached, but in a set of symbols.[13] At the center of every religious tradition is a symbolic complex as the primary, indispensable, normative expression of the constitutive content of the tradition. Propositions are derivative expressions. They have a place, because the central set of symbols embodies meaning in a compact, undifferentiated fashion, like a work of art. Propositions unpack the meaning of the symbolic complex and are related to it in the manner in which a critical analysis is related to a poem or a play.

The reason why the objective core of a religious tradition is a set of symbols, rather than a body of concepts and propositions, is the nature of religious faith. Faith is not a detached intellectual assent, but the adoption of a fundamental stance in life. It is the choice of a basic attitude to reality, with a corresponding way of life; in other words, it is a fundamental option embracing one's total being and personality. That kind of commitment is not mediated through conceptual analysis or detached argumentation, but through symbols as dynamic images evoking a personal response.

Religious faith cannot be handled purely intellectually. It arises in consciousness at the level of freedom and conscience, and depends upon the fundamental personal orientation of the individual and the group. At that level the horizon within which people think and act is the result of their free decisions. To say this does not exclude an intellectual element and a need for objectivity. Correct religious judgments and decisions demand sufficient deliberation, and both conceptual analysis and factual gathering have a place in the deliberative process. Nevertheless, religious truth and values are not grasped by a detached intelligence, but in and through a personal, self-involving response. So, when deliberation passes over into evaluation, the soundness of the religious judgments and decisions depends upon the qualities of the subject. To put it in another way, religious assertions are not logically neutral, but self-involving.[14] For any understanding beyond the merely verbal they require that men should personally have had various depth-experiences, and of their nature religious assertions as made in the concrete express not impersonal knowledge, but the being, freedom, and virtue of the believer.

Moreover, in the matter of faith all of us have a starting-point, namely the tradition in which we were brought up. The intelligent and indeed only workable course of action is not to try to find some fresh, unquestionable starting-point, but to begin where we are. Descartes' procedure of attempting to establish an invulnerable initial certitude, a cognitive absolute, the *Cogito,* from which all our knowledge could be rebuilt, is simply a secularized version of revelation. It comes from the same false yearning after a datum immune from criticism with a ready-made objectivity and universality. There is no such starting-point; everything is subject to criticism. So, at the stage of development when one begins the work of self-appropriation and turns away from an unexamined life, one finds oneself with a mixed inheritance of convictions and attitudes, judgments and decisions, ideals and values. The process of sifting these is slow and arduous. There is no shortcut, though some changes do bring about a complete restructuring of one's subjectivity. With religious faith the process of personal, critical appropriation can only be through action as well as thought. Only by the attempt to live out its implications to the full can we put ourselves in a position to modify, develop, or replace a fundamental option such as faith. Authentic as distinct from nominal faith cannot be changed from the outside, but only by entering fully into it, whether this leads to its confirmation or repudiation.

What, then, does it mean to be a Christian today without being a fundamentalist? This is how I personally see it: I am a Christian because the Christian tradition, with its symbols, doctrines and values, with its communities and institutions, has in fact mediated for me an experience of transcendent reality and has opened for me a level of consciousness and way of living I recognize as valuable and liberating. I find much truth and value in it. At the same time, much in the Christian tradition, indeed nearly everything as at present formulated, raises questions in my mind to which I have only tentative answers. In that sense I am full of doubts. But the Christian tradition is my religious starting-point. In trying to live it to the full, I have been compelled considerably to modify the faith as I inherited it, but I have not yet been led out of it into the adoption of some other fundamental stance or project for life.

Where—to come back to our main theme—does that leave the certitude of faith?

First of all, faith is not personal self-assurance or the warding off of feelings of insecurity. It is a self-transcending, trustful love of God—an attitude in itself very difficult for those who are for some reason or other psychologically insecure. I have given a theistic formulation of faith, but an equivalent attitude of trustful commitment to Ultimate Reality is found in other forms of religion. And religious faith in general is not designed for the insecure.

Again, the certitude proper to faith comes unsought and only unsought. The reason is that the basic certitude in faith belongs to it, not as an intellectual assent, but as a self-transcending relationship with God or Ultimate Reality, a relationship analogous to love. Love on the human level does not exclude an element of rational reflection and a need for objectivity. Those who think it does learn otherwise through broken marriages and unsuccessful friendships. All the same, the basic assurance of not being deceived in a situation of love is grounded upon the experienced reality of the loving relationship, not upon explicit argumentation. The certitude is reached, not by directly seeking it, but as a consequence of the loving relationship as a lived fact. It is the same with faith. Its basic certitude cannot be directly achieved by appeal to reason or authority; it comes from living out the self-transcending relationship with God which constitutes faith.

Fundamentalism misplaces the basic certitude of faith. Faith, we can agree, is of its nature wholehearted and not tentative. No fundamental option or project for life can be pursued halfheartedly without denaturing it. To live out any faith is a total enterprise.

That is why faith is associated with absolute certitude. But ambiguously so. Faith does not intellectually give absolute certitude.

Intellectually, the objective content of faith finds expression in propositions. These propositions participate in the basic certitude of faith on the scale of their importance in mediating its core relationship. They, therefore, vary in their degree of certainty or probability. I do not exclude that a believer may reach certitude concerning some of them.

Two points, however, should be noted concerning the certitude of religious assertions. First, the certitude remains a limited, human certitude. Certitude for men excludes only the fact, not the possibility of error. The believer in being certain of a doctrine is sure he has grounds for excluding error in that particular instance. He can make no claim that excludes error in principle as impossible. In religious matters as in others we have as human beings to live with the possibility and recurrent fact of error. Second, since the certitude of religious doctrines is derived from their function of mediating the central relationship of faith, the richness or poverty, the firmness or weakness of propositional belief will inevitably depend upon whether or not there is an effectively functioning, socially established symbolic order. When such an order flourished in the Middle Ages, a fine array of doctrines from the Trinity to guardian angels was firmly believed. Nowadays, on the contrary, for his faith the believer depends largely upon individual experience. All socially established systems of mediation have become precarious and unstable. For that reason his propositional beliefs are less extensive and less certain. Individual attempts to bolster their certitude will for the most part be in vain.

To conclude: lust may be defined as the seeking of the certitude of love by someone who is loveless. But the seeking is self-defeating. Only when the person no longer seeks his own reassurance, but accepts the risk of loving another, will he gain the assurance he otherwise vainly seeks. Since faith is a form of love, the direct pursuit of religious certitude is likewise lust. I suggest that it is lust of a particularly destructive kind.

NOTES

1. Yves Congar, O.P., *Jalon's pour une théologie du laïcat* (Paris: Editions du Cerf, 1953), 64–79; Eng. trans., *Lay People in the Church,* revised edition with additions by the author (London: Geoffrey Chapman, 1965), pp. 42–54.

2. Hans Küng, *Unfehlbar? Eine Anfrage* (Zurich-Einsiedeln-Köln: Benzinger, 1970); Eng. trans., *Infallible? An Inquiry* (Garden City, N. Y.: Doubleday, 1971).

3. Brian Tierney, *Origins of Papal Infallibility 1150–1350: A Study on the Concepts of Infallibility, Sovereignty and Tradition in the Middle Ages,* Studies in the History of Christian Thought, VI (Leiden: Brill, 1972).

4. *Revue des sciences philosophiques et théologiques,* 56 (1972), 650–53.

5. Paul Tillich, *Dynamics of Faith* (New York: Harper Torchbook, 1958), pp. 52–54.

6. Cf. Owen Barfield, *Poetic Diction: A Study in Meaning* (London: Faber and Faber, 1952). For a brief exposition, see "The Meaning of the Word 'Literal' " in L. C. Knights and Basil Cottle, eds., *Metaphor and Symbol,* Proceedings of the Twelfth Symposium of the Colston Research Society (London: Butterworth's Scientific Publications, 1960), pp. 48–63.

7. For a recent essay in interpretation, see Richard Schacht, "Kierkegaard on 'Truth is Subjectivity' and 'The Leap of Faith,' " *Canadian Journal of Philosophy,* 2 (1973), 297–313.

8. For a critique along those lines, see Paul Edwards, "Kierkegaard and the 'Truth' of Christianity," *Philosophy,* 46 (1971), 89–108.

9. In particular, Peter Berger and Thomas Luckman, *The Social Construction of Reality: A Treatise in the Sociology of Knowledge* (Garden City, N.Y.: Doubleday, 1967). For the application of the same principles to religion, see Peter Berger, *The Sacred Canopy: Elements of a Sociological Theory of Religion* (Garden City, N.Y.: Doubleday, 1967), and also his *A Rumor of Angels: Modern Society and the Rediscovery of the Supernatural* (Garden City, N.Y.: Doubleday, 1970).

10. Peter Berger, *A Rumor of Angels,* p. 50 (author's italics).

11. Cf. Leszek Kolakowski's stimulating essay, "The Priest and the Jester" in his *Marxism and Beyond: On Historical Understanding and Individual Responsibility* (London: Pall Mall Press, 1968). For the notion of revelation, see pp. 39–45.

12. Peter Berger, *The Sacred Canopy,* p. 187. See also his caustic essay, "A Sociological View of the Secularization of Theology," *Journal for the Scientific Study of Religion,* 6 (1967), 3–16.

13. For an elaboration of this thesis, see my book, *Christ and the World Religions* (New York: Herder and Herder, 1971), pp. 104–118.

14. Cf. Donald D. Evans, "Differences Between Scientific and Religious Assertions" in Ian G. Barbour, ed., *Science and Religion: New Perspectives on the Dialogue* Forum (New York: Harper Forum Book, 1968), pp. 101–133.

II

COSMIC VANITY

Probably anyone who has been in the public eye on some religious matter has had the same experience as myself of receiving a stream of literature from fringe religious groups. A theme occurring fairly often in this strange material is the claim to a privileged knowledge of the origin, structure, and workings of the cosmos. For example, there comes to my mind a large, expensively, produced volume with maps, diagrams, and tables, presenting a complex cosmology with confident detail.

Not for a moment did it occur to me to take that sort of stuff seriously, and most people would react in the same way. But I was led to ask why, if I dismissed those fringe cosmologies so brusquely, I should continue to pay attention to the cosmological views found in the major religions. Were they any better grounded than the fringe cosmologies? Were not all religious claims to a knowledge of the origin or structure or workings of the cosmos equally illegitimate?

An immediate difference makes one hesitate to say Yes. The fringe cosmologies are the product of individuals or of small aberrant groups, whereas those of the major religions come from great social traditions with long histories.

The function of the great cosmologies in the social ordering of human experience and thus in the social construction of knowledge gives them an objectivity marking them off from the subjective projections of imaginative individuals or of socially marginal groups. The same can be said of the social function of cosmologies embedded in the so-called primitive religions or preliterate peoples. We cannot, therefore, summarily dismiss all religious cosmologies, but must examine their meaning more closely. Nevertheless, my contention is that the strange, luxuriant cosmologies of the religious fringe are only crude instances of yielding to a temptation that dogs all religion and leads to less obvious sins in the major religious traditions. That temptation I will call the temptation to cosmic vanity.

The vain man assumes that the world is as he sees it and also takes for granted that others should see things the way he does. He acts as though his own outlook were universal and objective and is indignant if others do not share his outlook. Cosmic vanity occurs when men impose their social structure upon the cosmos as a whole, falling into the conceit of interpreting the entire cosmos in terms of the limited preoccupations and organization of a particular society and culture.

Thus, when in the Middle Ages society was established as a fixed, hierarchical order with predetermined relationships, the cosmos was conceived in a parallel fashion as a static order in which every rank of being had its appointed place. Now that society is subject to constant change, and relationships within it are fluid and unstable, the cosmos is conceived as a dynamic process. Confidence in the progress of human society was soon given its counterpart in an evolutionary cosmology. Likewise, the caste system of Indian society was seen as founded upon the structure of the cosmos in Hindu mythology.

But it would seem that I could here go on to cite all the cosmologies. Are not they all centered upon man and does not each reflect a particular society? In short, does not a rejection of cosmic vanity rule all cosmologies—at least religious cosmologies—out of court?

There is a problem here of interpretation. To handle it successfully, something must be said about the origin and function of cosmic representation in religion, and to do that we must first consider myths or sacred stories in general.

I said in the previous chapter that at the center of every religious tradition was a set of symbols. I could have said a series of stories, because the symbols in question are not static representations like statues, but dramatic images, grouping and deploying themselves in narratives. The complex of symbols at the heart of every religion takes the form of sacred stories or myths.

Let me begin to elaborate this with a few words about storytelling and human experience.

Raw experience is chaotic—a confused, tumbling mass of discrete impressions, images, sentiments, and physical reactions. Experience in that sheer state, that is, unordered and unpenetrated with any principle of meaning, is rarely met with in an adult. Language itself is a trelliswork of meaning, and a particular language is a particular way of ordering experience meaningfully. As the child learns to talk it learns to blend raw experience with intelligent meaning and mold it into significant patterns.

To envision brute experience unformed by meaning we have to consider those extreme instances where a collapse occurs of the entire structure of meaning for a person or a society. It is possible for the world of a society or of an individual to disintegrate and crumble into dust. A loss of meaning takes away all pattern, purpose, and intelligibility from the process of social or individual living. Experience, social or personal, no longer makes sense. A society overcome by loss of meaning is wrecked by disorder and the clash of group interests until a new order is created by new meaning or the society is absorbed in the order of another society. An individual whose world has collapsed, for example through the death of a significant person or the failure of a career, wanders bewildered through the kaleidoscopic whirl of continuing experience until some more powerful source of meaning is found, able to unify his life, including the negative elements, into a significant pattern.

Human life, therefore, demands that we lay hold of our experience, interfuse it with intelligent meaning, order it into some kind of pattern and thus make sense of it. But how do we do this?

Well, we do not do it in the first place by producing theories and systems. The emergence of theoretical, systematic intelligence was a legitimate development of human consciousness, and the world of theory it has created has its place and function among the elements and levels of our complex human living. But men as a rule do not live by theories even in this scientific, technological age. When a scientific theory, such as evolution, becomes a basic view of life, it changes its nature. It no longer functions as a theoretical formulation of limited scope produced and controlled by scientific intelligence, but as a symbol of vaguely determined and wide-ranging meaning under the impetus of man's ideals and hopes. Theories and the technical concepts and language they demand have their part to play in the ongoing development of human knowing and thus in human living, but it is not their function to provide the primary ordering of raw experience.

The basic way we order our experience and permeate it with meaning is by shaping it into stories. Intelligence first uses the story when it lays hold of experience, molds it with meaning into patterns and gives it sense and order. And storytelling remains fundamental, underlying other forms of discourse. A story arranges the jumbled mass of experiences into a sequence. It links events together, establishes connections among actions, relates persons to one another as actors in the story sequence. A story in that fashion provides a single frame of meaning for a diversity of experience.

Everyone in a general way knows what a story is, but it might be helpful to point to some of its structural elements.

A story is a narrative. The narrative line is the sequence through which the events, the persons, and their actions are interrelated. The unity of a story comes from its having a beginning, a middle, and an end. The beginning is a point where no earlier event is needed to understand the narrative that follows. The middle tells the events leading to the end. The end is the outcome; it gives us the resolutions or at least the result of the narrated events.

To the extent that a story reflects the contingency of life, the end is unpredictable, though acceptable when it comes. We criticize a story if the ending is far-fetched and does not seem a natural outcome of the narrated events and the characters of the persons involved. On the other hand, with a skilled storyteller the story almost to its close remains open to a number of different endings. When the ending comes we accept it as appropriate, but it was essentially unpredictable.

Finally in this account of a story: to create a story demands selection. No story arises by exhaustively recounting everything that happened in a given time. For a story a principle of meaning and organization is required, enabling one to select what is necessary for a particular pattern or story line. That is why a story is by its very nature and function a means of ordering our experience and permeating it with meaning.

Let us turn now from the concept of a story to the manner in which stories function to give our experience a pattern of meaning.

Individuals reach self-consciousness as persons in and through the community or communities to which they belong. The struggle for meaning on the part of an individual takes place in the context of the tradition of a community, even if personal growth leads eventually to the rejection of that tradition. Logically, therefore, attention should first be given to community stories. However, since the main theme of this chapter, cosmic vanity, concerns community stories, it is more convenient to deal here parenthetically with personal stories before getting into cosmic myths and the vanity they occasion. Besides, to see the functioning of stories on the personal level is helpful to many in grasping the nature and function of community stories or myths.

Within the framework of meaning established by stories fundamental to the community or communities to which he belongs, each person becomes the author of the story of his own personal life. We create and express our sense of personal identity by ordering our life experience into a story. Various events of our past experience are remembered and remain ordered in our mind in a narrative sequence. We make sense of our present by relating to our past, and both past and present are arranged so as to uncover future potentiality and direction.

Before death the story of our life is still in the making. It is, then, a story constantly retold and changed in the retelling. An event may greatly change our lives. When that occurs, past events are thrown into a different perspective and events previously forgotten are remembered and recognized as significant for our life history. A continuous retelling in a new way of our personal story is the normal requirement for growth. A crisis, however, arises if the story we have created breaks down under the pressure of new events, continuity is lost and events both past and present are scattered in a meaningless chaos. A new story has to be created in order to give a new personal identity, a new self-meaning.

While the life story of the individual is created in the context of the larger story of the community or communities to which he belongs, that life story is peculiarly his own and is not just identical with the story of his community.

At least, that has been so since the emergence of a sense of the individual in the first millennium before Christ, which resulted in the differentiation of human consciousness into an awareness of the self, or the interior world, and an awareness of the world over against the self, or the exterior world. Since then, for anyone who has reached a distinct self-awareness, a meaningful ordering of experience is not sufficiently achieved by intelligibly ordering the exterior world, namely the world of nature and of social reality. His own personal existence as a self in that world has to be made intelligible, and this is attempted in that meaningful pattern which for each of us takes the form of the story of his life.

All the same, as we saw in the previous chapter, even our inner life is dependent upon society, because it is created and sustained in a dialectical relationship with society. Now let us take up the question of community stories.

As a general rule a society embodies its common convictions and values, in other words its self-meaning, in a set of stories. Through the framework of meaning provided by these stories the community interprets and orders its ongoing experience. The stories are also the way the society accounts for and justifies its laws, customs, and institutions.

In most cultures fundamental community stories are sacred stories. This means they claim to give a comprehensive scheme of meaning rather than disconnected particular meanings and, to achieve this, appeal to some transcendent order of reality beyond the immediate and transitory.

To explain this I want to pick up again the notion of revelation, but this time without implying any a priori claim to objectivity and universality.

In order to create a story a unifying principle is needed—some central image or idea radiating meaning over all the events of the story and providing the light in which they are ordered into a pattern. Revelation occurs when some image or idea lights up for us and casts its illumination over the life of our community or over our personal existence. As a central source of meaning the revelatory image or idea brings all the diverse and apparently conflicting elements of social or personal living into an intelligible unity. It is revelation that determines the central symbols which give focus and direction to the ongoing life of the community or person and which display their full meaning and unifying power by being deployed in the dramatic narrative of a story.

The revelation serving as the source of meaning for the community stories has to become a source of personal meaning and create our individual stories. Usually it is some aspect of the community revelation which becomes revelatory for the individual in his personal existence. But there are occasions when what is seen by the individual in a blaze of illumination is so original as to constitute a new revelation and a new source of meaning. However, most of us build our lives upon a personal grasp of the revelation grounding the life of our community. It has to become a revelation for us, lighting up for us and radiating its meaning over our lives, giving them unity and purpose.

So far I have considered revelation as a source of illumination creating a comprehensive scheme of meaning for the community and the individual. But revelation is usually thought of as religious, and revelation is properly religious when it occurs within the transcendent dimension of human experience and illuminates the ultimate conditions of human existence.

Mention has already been made of the differentiation that has emerged in human consciousness between the interior world of distinct self-awareness and the exterior world over against the self. Another differentiation of consciousness, though longstanding, has become sharply explicit in recent centuries. It is between the world of ordinary experience, namely the world within man's observation, grasp and sometimes even control, and the world related to his experience of the boundaries of his existence, the world arising from his awareness of a beyond, transcending the finite being of himself and the limits of the everyday world to which he belongs. The world of ordinary experience is the profane world; the world beyond is the sacred world. These two worlds are closely interrelated. Any consideration of the ultimate conditions of the profane world confronts us with the question of the transcendent or sacred. On the other hand, the sacred is disclosed only in and through the profane world in its finiteness and symbolic power.

The twofold differentiation—between the interior and exterior worlds and between the sacred and profane worlds—represent, in my view, a gain. I should regard any attempt to return to a compact undifferentiation of consciousness as psychologically regressive and harmful. All the same, it is clear that something has gone wrong with the development. Many modern men feel cut off from the world around, as isolated selves, and the sacred has become so remote from the profane world as to be irrelevant and unreal. Indeed, the sacred is now ignored or denied by the secular men of today. The distortions of development are connected with the erection of modern science into an exclusive ideal.

Dominant and all-pervasive in modern culture are the empirical sciences. I include the social or behavioral sciences as well as the natural sciences. All the modern sciences share the common ideal of knowledge according to which genuine knowledge is reached by verifying possibilities, that is hypotheses, in the data of experience. Knowledge is concerned with the factual, and it rests content with finding out what is so as a matter of fact. It does not seek after eternal truths, absolutes, universal principles. Insofar as we can formulate abstract universal laws as in mathematics, these become tools for the investigation of the facts, namely what can be verified in the data of experience.

This kind of knowledge, which became the dominant ideal of Western culture from the time of the scientific revolution at the end of the eighteenth century, does not and cannot include the sacred. All the modern sciences are by the limits of their method secular. The sacred as such is not a datum in the sense used by modern science. Hence a method restricted to investigating what can be verified as contained within the data of experience, as immanent in those data, cannot reach the sacred in itself as transcendent.

In speaking of modern science as methodologically secular I am in no way attacking their validity and legitimacy within their own sphere. I should regard a scientist who introduced, say, God as a factor in an experimental report not only as a bad scientist but as a bad theologian. As an attempt to study contingent facts in themselves and in their mutual relations, the method of modern science is in place, and since God is not and should not be made a contingent fact there is no call to make any references to him. However, the almost exclusive dominance of modern science has led to a narrowing and distortion of human consciousness—not only of our knowledge about things but the manner of our awareness of ourselves and the world. The result has been that modern consciousness shaped by the empirical sciences is closed to transcendent experience.

The success of the empirical scientific method, both in pure science and in technology, led to the downgrading of other forms of experience and knowing. Not only faith and theology, but also philosophical reflection and artistic experience came to be regarded as subjective in the sense of having very little to do with the real world. Only science, it was thought, put us in touch with the hard facts, with the world as it actually was independently of our subjective desires, fantasies, and emotions.

But the change brought about has gone deeper than that. Science has altered the way we experience the world. Modern man does not merely think differently about the world from medieval man; he experiences a different world. There has been a shift in human consciousness.

Modern science has caused us to experience the phenomena of the external world as objects standing over against man, having their reality and consistency independently of human consciousness. Hence there is isolated self-consciousness on the one side and external objects on the other. Attention is paid exclusively to the objects in their supposed independent consistency in an endeavor to determine what are the objective facts. This experiencing of the world as a set of objects existing independently over against human consciousness creates the further problem that it does not open out onto an experience of the transcendent.

To put it in another way: the phenomena of the world are no longer seen as representations. By representations I mean phenomena experienced as bound up with consciousness and full of meanings. Men did not confront representations as bare objects, but they participated in them as expressions of man himself and as manifestations of hidden, transcendent reality. In brief, the phenomena were symbols, but not in the modern sense of having a meaning superimposed upon their literal fact. They were in their very consistency and reality expressive of the consciousness present in man and in the universe.

When the phenomena of the world were experienced in everyday life as representations full of human and cosmic meanings, then without forcing or difficulty the world could be perceived as sacramental or symbolic of the transcendent. It was not a question of imposing an added symbolic meaning upon supposedly independent, self-contained physical facts. Only the implicit assumptions carried by the scientific method have led men to construct the phenomena of experience into a world of so-called physical objects independent of the consciousness of the observer and deprived of any meaning other than their physical relationships.

Reality as a world of physical facts is, it must be stressed, the creation of the metaphysics accompanying the exclusive dominance of the empirical method. It would still be possible, without jettisoning modern science, to construct a different world. We could distinguish, but not divide objects from the conscious subjects perceiving them. We could consider the phenomena, not merely for limited purposes in a physicality stripped of all ulterior significance, but also more generally as representations, dependent upon consciousness for their full actuality and bearing multiple meanings. We should have, not a physical world over against man, but a world united to man in mutual participation. Such a world in being fully expressive of man would become a manifestation of the transcendent dimension of human experience, and thus a sacred symbol.

My conclusion is that modern scientific and technological culture has altered human consciousness in a manner that excludes the transcendent. Modern man has been led to perceive himself as an isolated self-consciousness in a world of physical objects thought of as fixed in space and time, standing free of human meanings and constituting the same world for all observers. Such a world of physical objects does not include the sacred nor does it carry any meaning leading to God or the transcendent. Since this world is presented as the real world, the only real world, somehow objectively out there, the sacred becomes unreal—God is dead.

What I am saying is that modern men do in fact live in a world without God, but unfortunately they are still unaware that this world is a world of their own construction, dependent upon the way they understand, construct, and thus perceive the phenomena of their experience.

I have said that revelation is religious when it occurs within the transcendent dimension of human experience and illuminates the ultimate conditions of human existence. The transcendent dimension of experience is that sense, perhaps vague or implicit, of the abyss or void that surrounds human existence. It is a sense of limits, but at the same time a sense that reality stretches beyond those limits. The dynamism of man's spirit, if not checked or suppressed, draws him toward that abyss. Vague intimations of enveloping emptiness as an inescapable feature of the human condition may be called pre-religious. Religious experience properly so called is when some revelatory symbol lights up the abyss as positively meaningful, disclosing it as powerful and loving reality. It still escapes our apprehension, remaining in that sense the nothingness beyond. But we feel ourselves grasped by it, enfolded into it as both ultimate reality and ultimate value, as both infinite power and infinite love. Hence the religious attitude at its most fundamental and most general is a positive openness to all reality with complete trust and confidence. Religious faith is a conviction of ultimate meaningfulness and a loving acceptance of total reality.

Religious faith does not exist in the abstract generality, but in particular concrete forms. These concrete forms of religion have their origin and ground in particular revelatory symbols, which are in fact embedded in stories.

So we return, with I hope greater understanding, to the statement that in most cultures fundamental community stories are sacred stories. Sacred stories are stories including the ultimate conditions of human existence in the meaningful pattern they create. Further, they find their source of meaning and unifying principle in symbols revelatory of transcendent reality. They in effect look to the transcendent as the final source of meaning.

As might have been expected, sacred stories do not always and for everyone exercise a revelatory power. The recitation of sacred stories is not sufficient to ensure the occurrence of genuine religious experience. Sometimes, indeed, sacred stories can become dead. Nevertheless, in most cultures, unlike in our own, the secular was not closed off from the sacred, and the structures of meaning for everyday life were explicitly related to the sacred. The life of the community was expressed and justified through sacred stories.

Sacred community stories are commonly called myths. The simplest definition of myth is a story of the gods. As now used in modern religious and cultural studies, the word "myth" designates any sacred story that expresses the self-meaning of a community and thus serves as a social charter. The word "myth" in that sense does not imply untruth. The question concerning the truth of the community stories is bracketed. Again, the word "myth" is nowadays often used for community stories, whether these are sacred or not.

A large proportion of the sacred stories of ancient peoples are stories about the beginnings of the cosmos. They tell of what happened in that primordial time before historical time when the cosmos as we now know it was formed. So prominent is the cosmogonical content of early myths or sacred stories, that we tend to identify myth with ancient cosmogony, though this is unduly to limit the meaning of myth.

Indeed, from an opposite point of view, we might well ask why religion should ever have been concerned with the formation of the cosmos. Nowadays we regard all questions about the manner in which the universe came into its present state as scientific and outside the province of religion. Is, then, the cosmological element in sacred stories to be dismissed as primitive science confused with religion? No, cosmic myth is not so easily disposed of. However, after the lengthy preliminary explanation I have given of sacred stories, a positive account of cosmic myth can be fairly brief.

Like all myths, cosmic myths as community stories are intended to legitimate and give meaning to the structure and life of the society. An obvious way of doing this is to relate the social order to the cosmic order and then attempt to give some account of the origin and nature of the cosmos. Human meaning as institutionalized in the social order is identified with the structure of meaning inherent in the cosmos itself.

Further, cosmic myths are designed to ground human existence upon transcendent reality. That the source of meaning is placed in the transcendent is shown by the placing of the mythical happenings and actions in a time outside time. Unlike with modern science, it is not a question of tracing cosmic processes back to a remote past in linear continuity with the present. The mythical time of the beginnings is outside the temporal flux. For that reason the mythical events could become present again in ritual celebration. Cosmic myths are not primitive science, but symbolic stories revelatory of ultimate meaning.

At this point an illustration might be helpful. For it I turn to the ancient civilization of Mesopotamia.[1]

The Mesopotamian view of the universe took shape at the same time as Mesopotamian civilization as a whole, namely around the middle of the fourth millennium B.C. At that early period the Mesopotamians lived in a primitive democracy where all important decisions were taken in a general assembly of all the citizens. In accord with the general principles I have outlined, the social order was transferred to the cosmos. The cosmos was, as it were, a vast state, and in the cosmic state the ruling general assembly was an assembly of gods. At this point the sacred symbolism of the cosmology becomes evident. The gods who constituted the divine assembly were powers the Mesopotamians acknowledged in and behind the various phenomena of nature. The literature shows that these powers, such as the sky representing authority, the storm seen as force, the earth associated with fertility, and the waters typifying an active creativity, were revelatory of sacred, awesome presence for the Mesopotamians.

That vision of the universe was formed at an early period, but a fully developed cosmogony, giving an account of the origin and structure of the cosmos, appears only in the first half of the second millennium B.C. We find it in a composition called the *Enuma elish*. In the form in which we have the work, the central figure is Marduk, the god of Babylon. This corresponds to the fact that Babylon was at that time the political and cultural center of Mesopotamia. When later, in the first millennium B.C., Assyria became the dominant power, Assur was substituted for Marduk. Further, there are indications that earlier Marduk himself replaced Enlil of Nippur. The myth was thus modified to meet changes in the political situation. Again, a more detailed interpretation of the myth confirms that society served as the model in conceiving the cosmic order. Observed facts about the physical origin of Mesopotamia itself would seem to be the basis for the account of cosmic origins, and knowledge about the origin of Mesopotamian political organization the basis for the speculations about the origin of the organization of the universe.

Over a long period in Babylon a New Year's festival was celebrated, lasting several days. During this festival the Babylonians reenacted the victory won by Marduk over the forces of chaos on that primordial New Year's day when the world was created. The *Enuma elish* was recited, and a mock battle was fought in which the king acted the part of the victorious god. The mythical events were thus made present ritually. They themselves stood outside of historical time, and in that way represented a transcendent source of meaning.

There are, then, two levels of meaning in cosmic myths. First, they are attempts to give rightness, permanence, and validity to the definitions, differentiations, and institutions of the social order by rooting them in the cosmos. The socially constructed world of human culture is always precarious. Understandably, men have struggled to give it some stability by relating it to the universal order of the cosmos. Second, the myths were an attempt to point to transcendent reality as the ultimate source of reality and meaning for society, and they functioned as sacred symbols.

Religious cosmologies are therefore doubly symbolic. They are the social order writ large upon the cosmos and then taken as manifesting transcendent reality.

It would seem to be natural to men to order and express their social and religious experience in the form of a cosmology. However, in doing so, it has been their constant temptation to suppose they were somehow privy to the secrets of the cosmos and able to give, not just a scheme devised from a human standpoint, but an objective picture of the order of the universe. I have called it the temptation to cosmic vanity.

Cosmic vanity, I suggest, is not of minor importance. On the possibility of avoiding it depends the answer to the question whether religion is intrinsically alienating.

The problem of the alienating effect of religion has recently been sharply raised by Peter Berger.[2] The context of his treatment is the legitimation of society provided by religion through a "cosmization" and "sacralization" of the social order, namely, through the insertion of the social order into a universal cosmic order regarded as sacred. Alienation, in Berger's sense, occurs when men lose the awareness that society is a human product; or, in other words, that social institutions are the creation of human activity. Men are alienated from society when they no longer recognize that society is their own product. In other words, the dialectical relationship between men and their social world is lost to consciousness. The essential difference between the socio-cultural world and nature is obscured. Human products are transformed into nonhuman, inert things, empty of human meaning; in brief, they are reified. As a consequence, the relationship between man and his world is distorted, and a false consciousness is produced. The consciousness is false because men, even while existing in an alienated world, continue to be co-producers of that world. Yet they do not apprehend the world as their own work, but as the work of some other—the gods, nature, fate. To quote Berger himself:

> Whatever may be the "ultimate" merits of religious explanations of the universe at large, their empirical tendency has been to falsify man's consciousness of that part of the universe shaped by his own activity, namely, the socio-cultural world. This falsification can also be described as mystification. The socio-cultural world, which is an edifice of human meanings, is overlaid with mysteries posited as non-human in their origins.[3]

So, as he maintains, religion has been a most powerful agent of alienation.

But is religion intrinsically and necessarily alienating? Not, I should argue, by its appeal to transcendent reality. Because the being, intelligence, freedom, and activity of men are rooted in ultimate, transcendent reality, the socio-cultural world precisely as a human product finds its ultimate meaning in the transcendent. In other words, an appeal to the transcendent does not, when rightly made, imply the superseding, diminishing, or doubling on a higher level of the free constructive activity of men. The transcendent is the ground of human free activity, not in any way its replacement or duplication. But such an understanding requires that the myths keep their symbolic, mediating role and do not become opaque by being misinterpreted as esoteric knowledge of the universe. If the temptation to cosmic vanity is not avoided, the myths cease to mediate a genuine religious faith in the transcendent. They are taken to be a second level of knowledge, with a consequent forgetfulness and denial that the cosmic order they picture is a human symbolic creation. When that happens, the proclamation of a cosmic order by religion becomes a potent cause of alienation.

At a prephilosophical state of culture one does not, as I have already noted, find the clear distinction between symbolic and literal expression, and consequently there is a naïveté of interpretation. But it would be a mistake to conclude that the cosmologies were taken literally in the sense of being given an absolute value. The anthropologist Mary Douglas, in her fascinating book, *Purity and Danger,* relates pollution and taboo to the social order and cosmic systems. In speaking of the Lele ritual of the pangolin, an anomalous beast that contradicts all the animal categories of the Lele, she says: "The Lele pangolin cult is only one example, of which many more could be cited, of cults which invite their initiates to turn round and confront the categories on which their whole surrounding culture has been built up and to recognise them for the fictive, man-made, arbitrary creations that they are."[4] Preliterate peoples could in their own fashion acknowledge the relativity of their symbolic cosmologies. No doubt, they could also fail to do so and become vain and inflexible in their cosmic speculations.

More useful for us, however, is to recall the trouble caused by cosmic vanity in Western culture. Before doing so, I will just remark that, having read some Buddhist authors who claim that Buddhism anticipated the findings of modern science on the origin and structure of the universe, I do realize that the temptation is not confined to the West.

Christians at first took over the biblical cosmology as the background of their religious teaching, but laid no particular stress upon it.

The cosmology of the Bible is merely an example of the views current in the ancient Near East, but adapted to Israel's belief in a transcendent God. The earth is flat and surrounded by water. The heavens, across which the sun, moon, and stars move, are enclosed by a solid cover, the firmament, half spherical in shape. Above the firmament is water, which comes down as rain through holes in the firmament. Below the earth is the realm of the dead. This cosmology forms the background of the Bible account and is presupposed in its language and images. But it is not given any great weight of religious meaning. God is said to be above the firmament, and yet he is not made part of the cosmic scheme. Again, what has importance for the biblical writers is not the structure or process of the cosmos, but its creation by God.

The Greeks developed a different cosmology. For them the earth was spherical and at the center of another sphere enclosing the universe. Between that outermost, enclosing sphere and the earth was a series of concentric transparent spheres, to which the various planets, including the sun and the moon, were attached. The stars were set in the outermost sphere. The earth was immobile, but the spheres moved around the earth, and thus caused the movement of the heavenly bodies. Within that general framework, Aristotle in the fourth century B.C. worked out the physical laws of the university, and Ptolemy in the second century A.D. developed a mathematical astronomy of great complexity.

When in the fourth century Christians came into closer contact with pagan learning, some opposed the different Greek cosmology in the name of the Bible. Lactantius, for example, ridiculed the Greek idea of a spherical earth, scornfully asking, Do the men at the antipodes walk upside down? Then in the sixth century Cosmas, a monk in the monastery of Sinai, though previously much-traveled, worked out a comprehensive cosmology on biblical lines in deliberate opposition to the Greek view. For him the earth is flat; its shape that of the Holy Tabernacle as described in Exodus, namely rectangular, and its length twice its width. The ocean surrounds the earth, and across the ocean and surrounding it is a second earth, the place of the Garden of Eden and the home of man until Noah, but now uninhabited. From the outer earth rise the walls of the universe. The roof or firmament is a half cylinder.

Some further details are added to take account of various biblical texts.[5] Thus, polemics and a somewhat literal mind led Cosmas into vanity.

The cosmology of Cosmas never became authoritative among Christians. There was in general no religious fuss about the structure of the universe. When after the Dark Ages a revival of learning came in the twelfth century, Greek science made its way without hindrance. By the thirteenth century the Aristotelian and Ptolemaic accounts of the cosmos were taken for granted by everyone of education, and Thomas Aquinas used the Greek cosmology in his great theological synthesis.

But now the cosmology created by pagan science, earlier opposed by suspicious Christians in the name of the Bible, was invested with a wealth of religious meaning. It became a cosmological representation of the Christian view of man and of the medieval Christian social order. The supreme expression of that symbolic cosmology is Dante's *The Divine Comedy.*

In Dante's epic the poet makes a journey through the universe. He starts on the surface of the spherical earth and travels through the nine circles of hell, which correspond symmetrically to the nine celestial spheres, descends to the innermost circle, the center of the earth and of the universe, the place of the Devil. He then returns to the surface of the earth at a point outside his point of entry and there finds the mountain of purgatory. He thus reaches the beginning of the celestial region. He travels through each of the nine celestial spheres, meeting the spirits who dwell in them. Beyond the ninth sphere he comes to the Empyrean, and there contemplates God's throne.

The structure is that of the cosmos of Greek science. The earth is at the center. It is surrounded by concentric transparent spheres, which carry around the planets and stars in circular motion. But the cosmology now expressed a religious world-view.

The place of man in the cosmos reflected his nature and destiny. He had a dual nature, material and spiritual, composed of body and soul. Being on the surface of the earth he was in an intermediate position in what was conceived as a hierarchical chain of substances stretching from the grossest kind of matter at the center of the earth to the spiritual substances of the higher celestial spheres. He was likewise intermediate between heaven and hell, between good and evil, faced with the choice of following his lower, bodily inclinations down to hell or his higher, spiritual aspirations up through the celestial spheres to God.

In brief, the cosmos of Greek science became the symbolic setting for the Christian drama of sin and salvation. A religious cosmology was formed in which men in a hierarchical world worked out their salvation or damnation in the sublunary region between angels above and devils below. No wonder the Copernican revolution and the rise of yet another new cosmology, a development that ran from Copernicus through Galileo, Tycho Brahe and Kepler to Isaac Newton, caused a religious upheaval. The earth was removed from the center and became a moving planet. Even more upsetting, the universe was no longer seen as finite and enclosed, but as boundless. There was now no center at all, so that the very notion of an ordered, hierarchical series of substances and regions no longer applied.

The whole self-understanding of man, social as well as religious, was affected. So what was wanted was a discussion of the vision of man expressed in the new cosmology. That cosmology was by no means pure empirical science, free from philosophical and religious assumptions. Unfortunately, owing to a failure to discern and resist the temptation to cosmic vanity, the debate did not take place at the appropriate level. Instead, the older cosmology was defended as a factual, objective account of the cosmos, supported by religious revelation. All that churchmen succeeded in doing was to infect modern science with their own vanity and encourage it to make exaggerated claims for its knowledge.

Science today is not exclusively an attempt to gain critically tested, objective knowledge of the universe. Any such knowledge is severely limited and does not amount to a complete cosmology. But much of the self-understanding of modern men is expressed through science. From that standpoint science easily passes over into what Stephen Toulmin has called scientific myth[6] and also gives rise to science fiction. Meanwhile, since the breakdown of the medieval synthesis, there has been no successful joining of Christian faith and science in a unified cosmology. Religious people have generally been content to cling to remnants from the older cosmology.

Most recently we have had a brilliant attempt at a new cosmology by Teilhard de Chardin. He has taken the findings of astronomy, geology, palaeontology, and biology and joined them to the religious doctrines of God, Christ, redemption, sacred history, and the end of the world to form a comprehensive evolutionary vision of the universe.

What Teilhard has given, I would emphasize, is a religious cosmology. His synthesis is therefore a symbolic representation of man's self-understanding and of his social and religious experience in an environment modified by science and technology, not a God's-eye view of the universal scheme of things. From a critical, theoretical standpoint, Teilhard has brought together diverse elements of all degrees of certainty and probability or none. To take but one example, I doubt whether the Pauline teaching on the cosmic Christ can be made absolute. Paul was rebutting a Gnostic subordination of Christ to cosmic powers. Within that framework of ideas Christ must be seen as supreme, but are we justified in giving Christ as man a universal function and supremacy in a differently conceived cosmos? Whatever Teilhard's own claims, to forget the relative and symbolic nature of any religious cosmology is to have learned nothing from the breakdown of the medieval synthesis.

But perhaps too much has been made of the theoretical flaws in Teilhard's synthesis, so that the reason for its weakness even as a religious cosmology has been overlooked. That reason, I suggest, is its lack of a social basis. An effective cosmology reflects the social order, symbolically extending its definitions and differentiations. Such a cosmology represents, strengthens, and clarifies the social and cultural world, creates, as it were, cosmic space for it, and so enables men to come to self-understanding. Against his will, Teilhard as a religious thinker was kept on the periphery of the social and ecclesiastical structure. Is that not why his cosmology has the uncontrolled exuberance, the optimism, and the air of unreality we associate with the ideas of millennialist groups, characteristics which with them are due to their lack of integration into organized society?

Teilhard was right in wanting an evolutionary cosmology. Modern evolutionary cosmologies alone correspond to man's present experience of continuous social change and cultural relativity or, in short, to the new awareness of what is now fashionable to call man's historicity.

But for any such evolutionary vision to have the accent of reality, it must reflect the concrete categories, distinctions, and relationships of the actual social order. Modern society, however, is fragmented and individualistic. Capitalism has encouraged individual aggrandisement at the expense of social cohesiveness and community values. The mentality it has created excludes any unified vision of reality. For that reason our society has not produced a clearly delineated and stable cosmology. Science fiction instead of cosmology has become the chief outlet for man's sense of a cosmic dimension to life and reality. Aspiration and fantasy have taken the place of certitude and reality.

Further, the separation of the profane from the sacred in modern culture and the reduction of the phenomena of experience from representations full of meaning to bare physical objects have undermined the use of cosmic images as symbols revelatory of the transcendent. The return to a religious cosmology demands a major cultural shift.

Meanwhile, the churches have been reluctant to accept man's experience of change and relativity. They have a nostalgia for a past static society and a universe of unchanging essences and absolute truths. Divinely established institutions, immutable natural laws, a canon of inspired Scripture, unchanging dogmas, creeds and rites —all these are remnants from an older cosmology.

Man has to make a home in the cosmos; he does not know its secrets. Cosmic vanity or the overevaluation of a past cosmology is hindering the churches in working for the new social order now needed and in creating a new cosmology that would set such an order in a wider vision of reality and link it to man's ultimate concern.

NOTES

1. I have drawn upon the account by Thorkild Jacobsen in H. and H. A. Frankfort, John A. Wilson, Thorkild Jacobsen, *Before Philosophy: The Intellectual Adventure of Ancient Man* (Harmondsworth: Penguin, 1964), pp. 137–234.

2. Peter Berger, *The Sacred Canopy, op. cit.,* pp. 81–101. For a penetrating discussion whether Berger's theory of religion and alienation is fully coherent, see Van A. Harvey, "Some Problematical Aspects of Peter Berger's Theory of Religion," *Journal of the American Academy of Religion,* 41 (1973), 75–93.

3. Berger, *The Sacred Canopy,* p. 90.

4. Mary Douglas, *Purity and Danger,* Pelican Anthropology Library (Harmondsworth: Penguin, 1970), p. 200.

5. See Arthur Koestler, *The Sleepwalkers: A History of Man's Changing Vision of the Universe* (Harmondsworth: Penguin), pp. 93–94. The book is an excellent account of the history of cosmology in the West.

6. Stephen Toulmin, "Contemporary Scientific Mythology" in Stephen Toulmin, Ronald W. Hepburn, Alastair MacIntyre, *Metaphysical Beliefs: Three Essays* (London: SCM Press, 1957), pp. 11–81.

III

THE PRIDE OF HISTORY

The next temptation, pride of history, would at first seem to be ill chosen. Is not the rejection of history, rather than any pride in history, characteristic of the religious man?

Mircea Eliade is perhaps the outstanding exponent today of studies in comparative religion. In his book *Cosmos and History*,[1] he describes how men of archaic and traditional societies, that is all premodern, which means religious, men, rejected history as a mode of existence and sought to annul it in their rites and myths.

Men of archaic societies found constant regeneration through the ritual repetition of actions regarded as archetypal and as establishing the pattern of their society as an unchanging order.

We have seen, for example, that the Epic of Creation called the *Enuma elish* was recited each year in Babylon at the New Year festival. The purpose of the annual ritual was the renewal of the permanent cosmic and social order. On the Polynesian island of Tikopia annual festivals reproduce the "works of the gods," namely, the acts by which the gods made the world as it is today. The ritual actions, repeating the mythical events, are in fact the same as the actions of everyday living, except that they are performed on only a few objects and are done with an intense sense of the sacred. In that way the archetypes behind ordinary life are made present ritually, thus renewing and confirming the existing pattern of society.[2] In New Guinea, when a captain goes to sea, he impersonates the mythical hero Aori, wearing his costume, performing his dance, and imitating his other actions. He sees his voyage as reproducing the archetypal voyage of myth. Again, archaic healing rituals usually include a solemn recitation of the cosmogonic myth, incorporating for the occasion a mythical account of the origins of the medicines used. The regenerative power or healing efficacy of the rites is seen as coming from their reactualizing of archetypal beginnings.

In brief, according to Eliade's interpretation, men of archaic societies strove to abolish history and live in an a-temporal present. He uses the phrase "archetypes and repetition" to characterize their culture and mentality. They refused change and history by constantly repeating mythical acts, intended as paradigms of an unchanging social order.

A change of outlook in regard to the repetition of cosmic events occurred in the traditional societies of the great early civilizations, notably in India. The repetition lost its power of regeneration for men of these cultures. As a consequence we have the concept of a cyclic time empty of meaning. Elaborate schemes of cycles within cycles of ages were worked out in the Hindu and Buddhist traditions. There was an eternal return of everything through endlessly recurring cycles of time. It was a terrifying vision, causing despair. Men sought release from the infinite meaningless repetition. Here again, though in a different fashion, there was a refusal of history and the seeking of present meaning outside history, whether through the *moksha* (liberation) of the Hindus or the nirvana of the Buddhists.

Even Christians, as we shall see more in detail in a moment, with their linear conception of time sought meaning beyond history through eschatology, namely the placing of a transcendent fulfillment of human existence at the end of history.

Only modern man, Eliade says, embraces history. He consciously and deliberately sets out to create it. Indeed, modern man sees himself as creative only as historical, because he insists in placing the source of his creativity in his own freedom. He claims the freedom to make history, because he lives autonomously as a historical being who freely makes himself.

Eliade, then, gives us a contrast between religious man of archaic and traditional societies on the one hand and, on the other hand, modern, postreligious man, who glories in his own autonomy and historicity, satisfied with the immanent meaning he can create within his own historical existence.

This, so it seems, would make the temptation to the pride of history a temptation to reject religion, so that such pride would be a characteristic of secular, not religious, men.

Moreover, the longstanding religious warnings against such pride would seem particularly in place today. "Modern man's boasted freedom to make history," writes Eliade, "is illusory for nearly the whole of the human race."[3] That is a point of which we are now becoming acutely aware. But even for the few privileged nations of the Western world, the time of reckoning is near. Far from being universally achievable in a general human progress, the present affluent style of living of the West is inevitably coming to an end, so we are being told, through population pressures, limited resources, and environmental pollution. The present is destined to become a past golden age. So much the worse, religious people might say, for secular man's pride in his freedom to make history.

Is, then, the appropriate contrast one between religion and secularism? Does it make any sense to speak of pride of history as a religious temptation?

However, the issue, in my opinion, is more complex than a simple rejection of religion.

Let us look again at the religion of archaic societies. This took the established social order and made it paradigmatic and therefore unchangeable. Ritual repetition of key features constantly renewed the validity of the social structure. Myths placed the origins of social institutions in a primordial, metahistorical beginning, and so made them symbolic of transcendent meaning. But in fact the social order was of human origin, historical and subject to change. To the extent that its relativity was forgotten—and it was not always overlooked—archaic religion created a false consciousness and became an alienating force. Men were alienated from the product of their own social and cultural activity; the symbols became opaque and idolatrous.

I would argue, then, that insofar as archaic religion was antihistorical rather than merely in search of metahistorical meaning, it was a refusal of men to accept the precariousness of their finite and temporal existence. Humility is truth; and truth liberates, not alienates. The denial of history in archaic religion was achieved only by the proud if frightened exaltation of a human, historically created social order as absolute.

This suggests the need for a deeper analysis.

"Only faith," we read in the Epistle to the Hebrews, "can guarantee the blessings that we hope for, or prove the existence of the realities that at present remain unseen."[4] Faith, we might paraphrase the text, is the negative capability of living without a present apprehension of meaning in the assurance that there is meaning. Pride of history in its various forms may be seen as a refusal of the negativity or darkness of faith. It is the outcome of a desire for a humanly conceivable, humanly tangible, already apprehensible meaning for human existence.

History is man's own being as temporal and finite. Faith is the opening of man's temporal being to the transcendent. There are two ways of refusing faith: first, by rejecting temporality as man's mode of existence; and second, by closing that temporality against the transcendent.

The first, the antihistorical refusal of any meaning in history, is the deceptive form pride of history takes in cosmological, sacramental, and mystical types of religion. The cosmological and sacramental religions, like those of archaic societies, are tempted to avoid the difficulty of faith by supposing a set of social institutions to be outside the flux of history as permanent and unchanging embodiments of transcendent meaning, which is thus kept comfortably within reach. The temptation of the mystical type of religion, such as Hinduism or Buddhism, is to take refuge from history in a supposed a-historical innermost being of man, which is thus made absolute. In either case there is a proud refusal of the historicity of finite man's existence.

The second way in which faith may be rejected is more direct. It is the refusal of transcendent meaning on the ground that history has its own meaning. Man's temporal existence is closed off from the transcendent. The meaning sought for history is not merely in history, because of its openness to the transcendent, but of history as exclusively its own creation. This historicism—if I may hesitantly use an ambiguous word—results from yielding to the temptation to pride of history as it threatens the prophetic or historical type of religion.

That form of the pride of history is our chief concern in this chapter. However, to handle it successfully demands that I enlarge upon the view of history embedded in the Bible and developed in the Christian tradition.

Let me begin by returning to the discussion of community stories or myths.

In Western culture fundamental community stories are historical in form. They are gathered together in what has variously been called existential or internal history. This is history as experienced and interpreted by participating selves as their own, in contrast to history seen from the external standpoint of a detached observer. It is not a question of truth and falsity, but of different sources and criteria of meaning and importance. Existential history is, as it were, the memory of a community, and in it the concern is with *our* country, *our* fathers, *our* victories, *our* defeats.

That kind of history is found in textbooks for schoolchildren and in stories about the past found in popular culture. I remember a Comic History of England that I was very fond of as a boy. The illustrations were amusing, but the book had the serious effect of fixing in my mind the series of events that form the traditional history of England—1066 and all that. French society is still divided by conflicting interpretations of the French Revolution, because these cause the opposing groups to read French history differently.

Existential history usually expands into fictional narrative and drama. For example, the sequence of events forming the American story is supplemented in exuberant fashion by Western novels and films, and *Gone With the Wind* similarly supplements the story of the Civil War.

To use historical events as the material for the stories fundamental to the life of the community is a procedure derived—at least in the West—from the people of Israel. It is the continuation in a secular fashion of a cultural form originally represented by the Bible.

Israel broke with the cosmological culture of the surrounding nations by establishing its own social existence, not upon cosmic myths, but upon history. The origin and nature of the cosmos were not a matter of fundamental concern, but only of secondary interest. The later editorial placing of the creation accounts at the beginning of the Bible is here deceptive. Those creation accounts have in fact very little influence and almost no further mention in the rest of the Hebrew Bible.

For a source of meaning in its social life and for the legitimation of its institutions Israel looked to the historical events that had created it as a people from diverse tribal groups, namely the Exodus from Egypt, the Covenant of Sinai, and the Conquest of the Promised Land. These events of its own history were seen as actions of God and expressions of his will. In other words, the sacred stories which constructed a meaningful social order and human existence for Istael were historical not cosmic. Sacred history or the series of revelatory, saving events thus became Israel's social charter, embodying its religious self-understanding and self-legitimation as a nation.

Because sacred history as used by the people of Israel has the same function of a social charter as the cosmic myths of other peoples and because as sacred, the history, like myths, is an attempt to express the transcendent, some writers put it under the general heading of myth. It is historical myth as distinct from cosmic myth —which, it should be noted, does not mean that it is untrue, but that it has a deeper truth than that of external facts as seen from a neutral standpoint.

I myself sometimes wonder how far the great stress upon sacred history in recent biblical scholarship is a product of Protestant thought, finding in the divine process of history the mediation it rejected in the sacraments. That would be in line with earlier Protestant attempts to oppose prophet and priest in Israel's religion. Worth mentioning in this respect is that by the twelfth century, Joachim of Flora, the author to whom modern thinking about history has been traced, was already attacking the realistic interpretation of the sacraments. Rudolf Bultmann in our day has seen sacramental mediation as neutralizing eschatology. From another angle, Bertil Albrektson in *History and the Gods*[5] has gathered evidence to show a general ancient Near Eastern belief in divine acts in history and in a purposeful guidance of the course of events and has shown the danger of exaggerating the singularity of Israel's view of history.

I do not want to deny that sacred history was a key feature of Israel's religion, but I think we should remember how far the concepts we favor in biblical interpretation may reflect later preoccupations.

Again, linked with the stress on sacred history is the contrast commonly made between the linear view of time in the Bible and the cyclical view of other religions. To the biblical view is attributed the unique historical awareness of the West as compared with the East. Here again we might easily exaggerate. Joseph Needham in *Time and Eastern Man*[6] has shown the inaccuracy of including China in the contrast. Chinese culture was second to none in its historical awareness. That still leaves valid a contrast between the biblical view and the Hindu and Buddhist cyclical schemes. Nevertheless, it warns us to be careful. I myself think that the contrast between the linear and the cyclical views is often overdone. There is a sense in which they can be seen as expressing complementary features of human existence.

With those words of caution about the limitations of our schemes of interpretation, let us return now to the discussion of sacred history.

Revelation for the Christian community consists in various historical events. These have become sources of meaning, illuminating and unifying the life of a people into the intelligible pattern of a story, a sacred history. The story of that people, the people of God, was in its turn seen as illuminating and unifying the life of mankind as a whole. Christians took over the story of Israel and made it their own. For them, however, the central revelatory event came in Jesus Christ, in whom the definitive pattern or final story line was made clear.

Let us look more closely at the form in which we have the Christian story.

The story of Christ took its rise outside literature within popular tradition. It is in that sense a folk story. A difference between a folk tale and a literary story is that a folk tale more often than not exists in several versions. In a story that is an achieved piece of literary art, form and content are inseparably wedded, so that its translation into another language or its transference to a new medium, such as the cinema, is a new artistic creation. Folk stories are more flexible; they have been told again and again in various ways without any one version's becoming the definitive version. That is the case with the Christian story. It has been told and retold in a variety of ways. The existence of different versions of it goes right back to the New Testament itself. Biblical scholars today recognize that the Epistles and Gospels give us not one but several different pictures or stories of Christ.

The different versions of a story are concerned with highlighting different elements of its meaning. A story is not a chronicle, a list of disparate events in a merely chronological series. A story has a pattern, meaningful order, a narrative line. To tell the same story differently is to shift its meaning, to alter its emphases, to bring out what before was only implicit, to pass over what before was prominent. Images as used symbolically in a story are polyvalent—within limits they are capable of a variation of meaning. The total meaning of the Christian story cannot be limited to any one version. New situations and new experiences lead to its being told once more in a new fashion.

At this point, however, many will raise the objection: the story of Christ is the account of what actually happened, and so, how can there be variations in that account without admitting error and untruth into the Christian faith? Thinking of this kind has led to ingenious and elaborate attempts to harmonize every detail of the four Gospels so that not the slightest contradiction remains between their accounts.

That approach rests upon a misunderstanding. Moreover, taken to an extreme, it represents a refusal of history—an inability to accept cultural differences, together with the changes and chances of the historical process.

However, before underlining its mistake, let me admit the element of truth in it. As I have already said, Jewish and Christian sacred stories use history for their material; for their symbols of the transcendent they take historical events. But more is involved than the use of history as a convenient source of images and suggestions for sacred stories. That particular historical events were in reality —I mean in themselves, not just in our minds—visible embodiments of God's presence and action is included in the meaning of the stories. For that reason the Gospel writers are insistent upon the historical reality of Jesus, of his life, crucifixion, and resurrection. The Fourth Gospel, despite its exalted doctrine of Jesus as divine, lays great stress on his being truly man against some first heretical denials of his full humanity.

In general, that God has made himself known by his presence and action in the very reality of man's historical life is at the heart of the meaning of the Christian story. To make the Christian story fictional, to deny the historical existence of Jesus or suppose him to have been a deluded simpleton, would be to destroy not just the factual truth of the Christian story but its religious truth.

But religious concern with the historical reality of the events constituting God's self-manifestation to men is not the same as concern with facts after the manner of modern history. Modern history as a discipline deals with events in their concrete particularity and as related to antecedents and consequences in a human, social context.

To take the second point first. History as a modern discipline is not concerned with any transcendent meaning relating an event to God. One could say it is concerned with events as facts, not as representations. Transcendent meaning comes within its scope only as the experience and belief of men, and thus as having antecedents and consequences in a social context. No event is directly considered as an act of God. It is merely noted that some men experienced it as an act of God. The method of modern history limits it to what can be verified within the data it examines. This excludes statements about God, because God as transcendent is not contained within any created data. Briefly, the historian today when keeping within his methodological assumptions does not and cannot consider events as related to God, but only as related to one another on the level of everyday existence.

I also said that modern history deals with events in their concrete particularity. All history is indeed selective and tries to discern a pattern, but the modern historian does delight in describing particular events in their concrete details. He is not content with the general nature of the happening, but with the particular circumstances of its occurrence.

To put the matter briefly. When we say that modern history is concerned to recount "what actually happened," we imply, first, that it describes events in close detail and, second, that it relates them to antecedents and consequences in a social context.

The sacred stories of the Bible, although they draw upon historical occurrences, do not give history in that modern sense. The writers are not as a general rule concerned with the details of the events in their concrete particularity; at most such a concern is occasional and secondary. The attention of the biblical writers is focused upon the religious meaning of the events. Again, they are not much concerned with relating the events to their antecedents and consequences within a social context, but with relating them to a pattern of divine activity and purpose in regard to God's chosen people.

Let me illustrate what I am saying by the example of the Exodus.

The modern historian wants to know, as we say, "what actually happened." This means he wants to reconstruct the event in close detail and relate it to the social and political circumstances. What took place at the Red (or Reed) Sea? What effect did the weather conditions have on the attempts to ford it by Israelites and Egyptians? What political factors governed the flight of the tribes from

Egypt? Viewed from this standpoint, the biblical accounts are comparatively uninformative and seemingly confused and contradictory. The preoccupations of the biblical writers were different from those of the modern historian. They acknowledged the fact that a remarkable and unexpected escape against great odds had been made from Egypt across a watery barrier that had entrapped pursuing Egyptians. They saw in this event a powerful action of God, rescuing those he had chosen to become his people. That religious meaning was what was important for them. For that reason they described the event in imagery intended to bring out its meaning as an act of God. To interpret the imaginative detail of the biblical accounts as historical detail of the event is just a misunderstanding. The study of the several different accounts we have of the event shows that the descriptions were not concerned with the concrete particularity of the historical event but with its sacred meaning. That meaning includes the basic factuality of the event, but not the details of how it happened in the concrete.

Against this background we can now consider the lack of historical knowledge about Jesus.

Even from the standpoint of modern critical history the existence of Jesus is not in doubt, nor the time and place of his life nor the general lines of his teaching nor his crucifixion.

However, if the modern historian wishes to go beyond these generalities, he finds that the only sources at his disposal, apart from background material, are the Gospels and that these are not histories in the modern sense but presentations of the religious meaning of Jesus by believing Christians, written to support and nourish the faith and life of the Church. Moreover, writing for that purpose, the evangelists did not have the same concern with detailed historical accuracy as the modern historian. They gathered together material, stories and sayings, already in existence as shaped and modified for use in the life of the Church, and they arranged this material in an order and sequence of their own, to suit the particular doctrinal purpose each had in mind. It used to be thought, without sufficient reason, that the order of events in Mark, the earliest of the Gospels, was historical. Most interpreters now agree that Mark's arrangement is as much a doctrinal creation as those of the other Gospels. Little is achieved by an attitude of shocked surprise that the evangelists did not handle their material according to the criteria of modern historiography. Why, in any case, should we take those as absolute? Where the Gospels overlap we can observe how the evangelists altered their material to adapt it to their doctrinal purpose. Similar alterations had been made at an earlier date in the pre-Gospel material, so that behind each text in the Gospels is a history of interpretive handling.

Better, surely, to try to understand the nature of the Gospels than to lament that they are not the kind of documents we should like.

Because, then, of the limitations for narrowly historical purposes of the material at our disposal, we are unable to write a biography of Jesus. We do not know the length of his ministry, nor the sequence of events in it. We cannot follow the development of the personal consciousness of Jesus about his mission, nor delineate his personal understanding of his death. We are unable to do more than offer hypothetical reconstructions of his personal teaching as distinct from the form that teaching assumed as developed by the faith of the primitive Church.

To demand more factual history than that, to insist on replacing the weighing of probabilities with the assertion of certainties, to kick against the variations and vicissitudes of historical conclusions: that, as I have already suggested, is an attempt to avoid history as temporal finitude and remove Jesus from his cultural situation and from the chances of the historical process.

What we do have in the New Testament is the story of Jesus, presented as a sacred story of ultimate meaning for men. It is told in several versions as used by the first Christian communities to express their faith and give sacred meaning and order to their lives. The different versions help us to grasp different elements of meaning in the story and thus provide us with the variety of material required for us to retell the story in a version adapted to our own situation. As I have already said, the religious meaning includes the basic facts of Jesus as constituting an event in which God embodied his presence and action in human history. The elaboration of those facts in the Gospel tradition was, however, a work of religious interpretation of their meaning, not a reconstruction of the historical life of Jesus in its concrete detail. But it is the meaning, not the historical detail, that is relevant to the ordering of our human existence by faith.

Among the New Testament versions of the Christian story the Pauline kerygma has received much attention in recent decades.

The word "kerygma" is transliterated from the Greek. It means "that which is proclaimed," and it has become a favorite word for the Christian message with biblical scholars and theologians. The word refers in particular to the versions of the Christian story found in Paul and John.

The center of interest in the Christian story for Paul is the death and resurrection of Jesus. We are saved by Christ because he died for our sins and rose for our justification. We were sinners, subject to sin, death, and the law, in a world ruled by the devil. God sent his Son in the likeness of sinful flesh. Jesus entered our sinful situation, and by his sufferings and death overcame sin and annulled our condemnation. Risen from the dead and exalted as Lord, he has become the source of the Spirit, so that, receiving the Spirit we are made one with Christ and adopted sons of the Father.

In Paul's presentation of Christ no place is given to the public ministry and teaching: all interest for Paul was focused upon the death and resurrection and their meaning for salvation. When we turn to the Synoptic Gospels—Mark, Matthew, and Luke—we find they make central a concern missing in Paul, namely, a concern with Jesus as bringing salvation in his words and deeds during his historical ministry. Precisely that concern created the unique literary form, the Gospel, which presents the historical life of a man as a decisive religious event—in other words, the public life of Jesus as the intervention of God for man's salvation.

Within their common concern each of the Synoptic evangelists offers a different account of Jesus.

For Mark, Jesus announces and brings the signs of the final Kingdom now about to come. A sense of urgency runs through his Gospel. The Kingdom is even now breaking in upon the world in the words and works of Jesus.

Matthew and Luke took over Mark, but modified his understanding of history for their own purposes.

Matthew has a particular interest in the organized life of the Christian community and is concerned with the question of the continuity of the Church with Judaism. His problem was this: the Law of God given to Israel was eternally valid, and yet Jesus was the final agent of God's purpose in the world. His answer was to present Jesus as founding the true Israel, the new community through which God's purpose would be achieved.

Luke, less concerned with the internal life of the community, wanted to give the Church its place in the history of the world. He highlighted the ministry of Jesus as a historical event, giving it a time and place among other known events. His approach to history, however, remains religious. He gives a division of history into periods according to a divine plan. The periods are three, namely: from creation to John the Baptist; the life of Jesus on earth; from the ascension of Jesus to his return. The third period is dealt with in the Acts of the Apostles, which forms one work with Luke's Gospel. Luke, therefore, has a positive interpretation of the delay in the return of Jesus in glory, and he sees both Jesus and the Church in the setting of world history.

For John the historical life of Jesus is revelatory of God and salvation. His emphases, however, are not those of the Synoptists. He presents the life of Jesus as the calm unfolding of a predetermined plan of God. The very death of Jesus is the moment of his glory, accepted beforehand by Jesus according to the will of his Father. John's understanding of history concentrates upon the present. He focuses upon the history of Jesus as provoking present decision and judgment. He does not concern himself with any future outcome or fulfillment. He does not deny the future events awaited by the early Christians, but what is important for him is the present decision of faith, which brings eternal life and judgment here and now. Consequently, John does not show any interest in the course of history or the unfolding of the ages, despite his stress upon the historical embodiment of God's presence and action in the life of Jesus.

There are other versions of the Christian story. In the New Testament itself there are traces of earlier forms of the story of Christ, and then there are other developed versions, such as the story of Jesus as high priest in the Epistle to the Hebrews. Christian tradition, shaping the biblical material into new forms under a variety of cultural influences, has constantly told the story of Jesus in new and different ways.

The existence of various versions of the story of Christ already makes it unlikely that any single, interpretive scheme for total history can be drawn from the Christian tradition. Can Christians claim to know the shape and meaning of world history? Is there, in fact, any final meaning governing the whole of human history from its beginning? Is history moving in a linear direction toward a final consummation, giving ultimate meaning to the historical process?

Despite its appeal to sacred history for its self-understanding and self-legitimation as a nation, only gradually did Israel acquire the idea of an absolute end to world history. The earlier forms of biblical faith tell of God's actions in history for some particular goal. There is no mention of any overall divine plan, embracing the whole of history and the cosmos.

This is true even of the prophets. Voegelin[7] distinguishes three phases of the prophetic hope. In a first, institutional phase Amos and Hosea looked for a better political order. The second phase he calls metastatic, because Isaiah, repeatedly disappointed with the king, placed his hope in a worldly transformation and the coming of an ideal political order, prepared for by a community of the righteous. Then with Jeremiah came the realization that God's purpose in history and the true hope of Israel could not be identified with any political order in this world. That was the third, existential phase, which focused upon the transformation of the individual soul. It reached its full expression in the Second Isaiah. The prophetic hope, though thus developing, remained a hope for the rule or Kingdom of God in history.

Eschatology in the full sense of the expectation of an absolute end of history emerged only when prophecy passed into apocalyptic under the influence of Iranian speculation.

Apocalyptic is a body of writing from the period 200 B.C. to A.D. 100. In a time of persecution and intense political frustration the apocalyptic writers looked forward to a definitive intervention of God in history, bringing this present world to an end and establishing a transcendent Kingdom. The expected intervention is described with exuberant imagery of cosmic destruction and renewal.

Unlike the prophets, these writers claimed to reveal the plan of God for universal history. They presented allegorical pictures of its unfolding and foretold the future course of history in its various stages according to a calculated time schedule. The sequence of events is seen as predetermined in the plan of God.

Since the writings of Johannes Weiss and Albert Schweitzer, biblical scholars have agreed in seeing Jewish apocalyptic as the background of the preaching of Jesus. Although the debate still continues about the precise content of Jesus' personal teaching, this may be described in general terms as a modified apocalyptic.

The teaching was apocalyptic, because Jesus announced the final, transcendent Kingdom in its imminent coming or its present realization or its breaking through already in anticipation—the phrases cover different interpretations.

It was a modified apocalyptic. First, Jesus rejected the apocalyptic attempt to calculate the time of the coming Kingdom. He gave no scheme of world history with a sequence of events determined by a plan of God. Second, he emphasized the inward and transcendent character of the Kingdom, the need for repentance and faith, the demand for personal decision. The resurrection of the body is affirmed; but the Kingdom is not identified with political events or cosmic upheavals. Third, Jesus avoided the exaggerated language and imagery found in apocalyptic writers. In these three respects he returned to the outlook and manner of the prophets.

The truth of Jesus' central claim to be bringing the final Kingdom was vindicated, in the faith of his disciples, by his resurrection. But his glorification prior to that of all men and without any transformation of the world forced a new understanding of the end. Previously in the apocalyptic expectation the coming of the Messiah and the end of the world were identified. For the first Christians the end now had two stages: the coming of the Messiah and the inauguration of the Kingdom in his personal resurrection; then, after an interval, the final consummation with the general resurrection and cosmic transformation. In between was an interim period in which Christians were now living. The last days had come; the final Kingdom was already present in an anticipatory fashion in the risen Lord; but Christians were waiting for the dissolution of this world and the open revelation of the Kingdom.

Understandably, the first Christians thought that the interim period would be short and the final revelation of the Kingdom not long delayed. "With the Lord one day is as a thousand years, and a thousand years as one day," was the reply of the Second Epistle of Peter[8] to those who wondered why the last days did not come. The possibility of a sense of imminence without chronological nearness is beautifully expressed also, centuries later, in this passage of John Henry Newman:

> Christ, then, is ever at our doors; as near eighteen hundred years ago as now, and not nearer now than then; and not nearer when He comes than now. When He says that He will come soon, "soon" is not a word of time, but of natural order. This present state of things, "the present distress" as St. Paul calls it, is ever *close upon* the next world, and resolves itself into it. As when a man is given over, he may die any moment, yet lingers; as an implement t of war may any moment explode, and must at some time; as we listen for a clock to strike, and at length it surprises us; as a crumbling arch hangs,

we know not how, and is not safe to pass under; so creeps on this feeble weary world, and one day, before we know where we are, it will end.[9]

Even so, not surprisingly, the urgent waiting and sense of nearness faded away. Christians settled down in a world that apparently went on as it had always done. They had to work out the problem of dealing with this world as though they had no dealings with it. The phrase comes from Paul. Here is the passage in full, because it describes well how Christians have to live in the world while waiting for its dissolution: "I mean, brethren, the appointed time has grown very short; from now on, let those who have wives live as though they had none, and those who mourn as though they were not mourning, and those who rejoice as though they were not rejoicing, and those who buy as though they had no goods, and those who deal with the world as though they had no dealings with it. For the form of this world is passing away."[10]

Two problems, however, emerged with the realization that the final revelation of the Kingdom was indefinitely delayed. The first, which arose already in New Testament times, is the problem of those who die before the final resurrection. The second is the problem of what the continuing history of the world might mean and how world history relates—if it does relate—to Christian hope for a transcendent end. Both problems are still with us.

If final salvation is to come at the end of history, what are we to make of death? Are those who die before the end to be deprived of that salvation? When the end did not come as soon as they expected, the first Christians were upset by the death of their relatives and friends. Paul reassured them in this passage:

But we would not have you ignorant, brethren, concerning those who are asleep, that you may not grieve as others do who have no hope. For since we believe that Jesus died and rose again, even so, through Jesus, God will bring with him those who have fallen asleep. For this we declare to you by the word of the Lord, that we who are alive, who are left until the coming of the Lord, shall not precede those who have fallen asleep. For the Lord himself will descend from heaven with a cry of command, with the archangel's call, and with the sound of the trumpet of God. And the dead in Christ will rise first; then we who are alive, who are left, shall be caught up together with them in the clouds to meet the Lord in the air; and so we shall always be with the Lord. Therefore comfort one another with these words.[11]

In short, do not worry about those who die. The coming of the Kingdom, which will glorify those who are still living, will bring the others back from the dead.

Nothing, however, is said about the interval between death and the final resurrection. It is metaphorically described as sleep.

Because of this hiatus, the doctrine of the immortality of the soul was introduced into Christian tradition from Greek culture. The immortal soul was then seen as reaching its destiny at death, going to heaven or hell, and the resurrection of the body became an inessential extra added later. However, the difficulty is that the immortality of the soul and the resurrection of the body come from two different stories, each story embodying a very different understanding of man. They cannot just be put together. Some elements of the immortality story might conceivably be combined with the resurrection story, but this has not as yet been done successfully. Recent writers have stressed that the resurrection story, unlike the immortality story, sees salvation as being given to the whole man, not just to a spiritual part, and as being social not merely individual.

Nevertheless, the early introduction of the immortality story shows that the resurrection story by itself does not present an adequate picture of human destiny. I have spoken of both as "stories" because that is what I think they are in their original form. Both, either singly or taken together, can serve as a starting-point for theoretical reflection that attempts to work out a conceptual statement of human destiny. How far such philosophical efforts can ever be successful is a different question. Whatever the answer, both religious accounts would be distorted if interpreted in the first instance as though they were theoretical statements and not imaginative, pictorial presentations.

The conviction, now firmly entrenched in the Christian tradition, that the individual attains final salvation at death clashes with a linear-historical view of salvation, placing it at the end of world history. It thus relativizes the import of sacred history taken as linear, and brings the Christian understanding of salvation closer than is generally acknowledged to the Hindu-Buddhist understanding, which sees salvation as a transition from history to a transcendent reality. The two views of salvation, in my opinion, still do not coincide. I should, however, want to hold that, though one-sided, the cyclical view of history symbolically expresses a valid insight about man's temporality as a perpetual perishing from which he seeks to be saved.

That brings us to the second problem: Does Christian hope imply a particular pattern for the continuing course of world history? Above all, does it provide grounds for asserting a general linear progress, despite vicissitudes, toward a final fulfillment?

History implies continuous change with no two historical situations being the same. A rigidly cyclical view is therefore antihistorical. Perhaps Nietzsche's insistence that we should joyfully embrace the eternal return of everything points to an inconsistency in the Indian outlook. An exclusively cyclical view in effect destroys the temporality of history and establishes it as eternal though moving permanence. It becomes unnecessary and incoherent to seek eternity and permanence beyond history in a transcendent reality or state. I have, however, already dealt with the form of pride that refuses the temporality of finite man's existence.

Our concern now is with a linear view, stressing man's temporality, but seeing history as moving toward a final achievement. What are the implications of the Christian story of the end of the world? History may be understood as the series of events constituting men's activities and development as social beings in this world. Does the Christian story imply that the course of history is a progressive movement toward a goal? In other words, does history viewed as a linear succession form a meaningful plan?

Have men, we may begin by asking, any reason to suppose that the fundamental conditions of human existence in this world can and ought to be radically changed? Men today, it would seem, are what they have always been and are behaving as they have always behaved, though with more powerful tools at their disposal. The ultimate problems defining the human condition seem much the same as they have always been: absence or threat of loss of meaning, spiritual ignorance, moral impotence, constant failure of attempts at self-liberation. Are there any grounds for saying that technological advance, while changing man's environment and consequently his immediate physical, sensory, and psychic experience, is also going to alter the deeper structures of his intellectual, moral, and spiritual makeup or solve the antinomies of the human condition?

At any rate, the Christian promise, I should maintain, is not that man can essentially alter his present temporal existence. That promise does not say that the final coming of the Kingdom will coincide with the highest point of historical progress. As far as the Christian story is concerned, the course of world history may be progressive or regressive, or alternately progressive or regressive, or completely irregular. The point of the Christian promise is that man's temporal existence is the context for faith in a transcendent fulfillment.

The apocalyptic imagery of the end of the world is a symbolic statement that ultimate meaning does not belong to history itself. When understood symbolically, not literally, it tells us nothing about the onward course of history or its chronological end. No more do the creation stories tell us anything about the chronological beginnings of the human race or the world.

To elaborate this:

The beginning par excellence for Israel was the Exodus and, inseparably connected with it, the Covenant given at Sinai. That was the beginning to which Israel looked back as founding its social existence. That was its chief source of meaning and order.

However, in the course of time the early folk traditions of the various tribes were gathered together, and the stories of the patriarchs, or ancestors, formed into a prologue of the history of Israel. The action of God in history for his chosen people was then seen as beginning with Abraham.

In a similar fashion some folk tales and creation myths, which came to Israel from the common culture of the Near and Middle East, were reworked by Israel to harmonize them with its faith in a transcendent God, and then they were attached to the stories of the patriarchs as a protohistory. The narrative of God's dealings with men, the line of sacred history, was thus carried right back to creation itself and the story of Adam and Eve.

Israel had come to a conviction that Yahweh was Creator of the whole world and Lord of universal history by grasping that as an implication of Yahweh's dealings with itself. God as revealed in the Exodus and at Sinai was a transcendent God. The vicissitudes of Israel's history drove home the point that God's power was not limited to any particular time or place. He exercised judgment upon the nations as well as upon Israel. The gods of the nations were as nought. Yahweh made this world and all that is in it. Israel's faith in God as Creator found magnificent expression at the time of the Babylonian exile in the writings of the Second Isaiah.

What we have in the creation stories of Genesis is Israel's faith expressed through an adaptation of elements from the cosmic mythology of the surrounding culture.

In handling the cosmic myths Israel presented them as a proto-history and thus fitted them into its own dominant cultural form, namely sacred history. This procedure, while putting the myths in a context meaningful for Israel, is misleading and has unfortunately misled. It gives rise to the wrong conviction that the material from which the first eleven chapters of Genesis are composed is historical. Granted that we do not anywhere in the Bible find critical history in the modern sense, we do in its main narratives have historical traditions religiously interpreted and presented as a manifestation of God's will. But the material substratum of the stories in the first chapters of Genesis, such as Adam and Eve or Cain and Abel, is not historical, even though like all myths the stories do reflect a particular cultural situation.

The literary form and context given to the stories about all mankind in the first chapters of Genesis made these stories into a protohistory—a series of preliminary, opening events in the narrative or sacred history. This was a literary device in order to subordinate these stories to the religion of Israel, which found its chief means of expression in historical narrative. But it is simply a mistake to suppose that God's act of creation was a historical act, somehow at the historical beginning of the universe, or to take Adam and Eve as historical personages who were in historical fact our first parents. These stories are to be placed in the everywhen of mythical time. They belong to the primordial beginning outside historical time. Hence these stories tell us nothing about what happened in the remote past or the cosmic process, but of what is permanently true of God, man, and the world. The story of the creation of the world tells us of its relation of total dependence upon God. The story of Adam and Eve tells us of the universal human situation.

I should insist that the eschatology, the narrative of the last events or end of the world, is to be interpreted in a parallel fashion to protohistory. Just as by the inner evolution of its own faith, Israel came to the conviction that God was Creator, so by a similar evolution it came to the acknowledgment that God's promise of salvation could not be identified with any earthly social and political order. Israel's hope, therefore, had to be interpreted as a transcendent and universal Kingdom. In expressing its deepened hope, Israel took over the Iranian mythology concerning a final cataclysm, just as it took over the cosmic myths for its expression of creation. The eschatological myths were in their turn adapted to Israel's dominant cultural form of history by being added onto sacred history as its final chapter. It is a mistake, however, to interpret eschatological events as though they were literally future historical events. They are events, like the events of cosmic myth, that occur in the everywhen of mythical time. The eschatological imagery, rightly interpreted, tells us nothing whatsoever about the chronologically last events of human history. Eschatology, like protohistory, is an expression of the universal human condition.

I can now finally state my main thesis. It is pride of history, I contend, that has produced various modifications of the Christian hope by making the end immanent instead of transcendent. Where the final goal has remained vague, the conviction of an immanent meaning in history has resulted in the idea of general progress—things are getting better and better. When the state of final perfection has been prominent without much thought of means, some form of utopianism or social idealism has been dominant. Finally, a full religious faith in the ultimate meaning of history itself has created the hope, as in Marxism, of the achievement of a perfect final order through the transformation of historical man.

The concept of history as a process of self-realization with an immanent goal derives, as I mentioned before, from Joachim of Flora in the twelfth century. Scholars are still exploring his role at the origin of the modern philosophy of history. Joachim dropped the Augustinian distinction between profane and sacred history and the parallel distinction between nature and grace. Those distinctions have often been misconceived as opposing two concrete orders, instead of being correctly taken as distinctions within a single total order. But if they are entirely repudiated, any hope transcendent to history itself is excluded. Man's temporality is then enclosed within itself and made divine.

On the other hand, the Platonic version of Christian hope, against which much modern thought is consciously reacting, evades the paradox, or negativity, of faith. History is man's temporality; and it is man's temporality—not some nontemporal element of man's nature—that is open to the transcendent gift. Man is entirely temporal and yet entirely saved. The resurrection of the body symbolizes this, in contrast to belief in the immortality of the soul. History from that standpoint does have meaning, though not necessarily a meaningful plan as linear succession. World history cannot be dismissed as a meaningless interlude coming before a juxtaposed end. But it is precisely because the reality giving meaning to history is transcendent, not a future historical achievement, that it is accessible as present meaning. It is neither a future historical state nor, except in symbol, posthistorical fulfillment, but present reality demanding faith.

History as a course of events is open-ended. Men might destroy themselves and their planet in the near future. They might, on the contrary, continue to build and work for many more millions of years. Whatever the case, intrinsically the human enterprise like the life of the individual is subject to death. Religious faith does not remove the fact of death, but it opens men in their temporal being to the transcendent. That openness carries with it a meaning that cannot be destroyed by death. The transcendent meaning offered to human existence is affirmed by faith in the face of death, without present apprehension or knowledge.

Religion, however, is always tempted to offer knowledge not faith. The dominant modern form of the pride of history offers, instead of faith, some humanly conceived plan of total history as saving "gnosis," or knowledge.

NOTES

1. Mircea Eliade, *Cosmos and History: The Myth of the Eternal Return* (New York: Harper Torchbook, 1959). See also by the same author, *The Sacred and the Profane: The Nature of Religion* (New York: Harper Torchbook, 1961) and *Patterns in Comparative Religion,* Meridian Books (Cleveland and New York: World Publishing Company, 1963).

2. Eliade, *The Sacred and the Profane,* pp. 86–87.

3. Eliade, *Cosmos and History,* p. 156.

4. Hebrews 11:1 (Jerusalem Bible).

5. Bertil Albrektson, *History and the Gods: An Essay on the Role of Historical Events as Divine Manifestations in the Ancient Near East and Israel,* Coniectanea Biblica, Old Testament Series I (Lund: CWK Gleerup, 1967).

6. Joseph Needham, *Time and Eastern Man: The Henry Myers Lecture 1964* (Royal Anthropological Institute of Great Britain and Ireland: Occasional Paper No 21, 1965).

7. Eric Voegelin, *Order and History. Vol. I Israel and Revelation* (Baton Rouge: Louisiana State University Press, 1957).

8. 2 Peter 3:8(AV).

9. John Henry Newman, *Parochial and Plain Sermons,* Volume 6, Sermon 17.

10. Corinthians 7:29–31 (RSV).

11. 1 Thessalonians 4:13–8 (RSV).

IV

THE ANGER OF MORALITY

I had occasion recently to reread the Catholic quartet of novels by Graham Greene, namely *Brighton Rock, The Power and the Glory, The Heart of the Matter,* and *The End of the Affair.* Thinking about them, I came to the conclusion that they revolved around a double tension Greene discerned in the Catholic system and outlook.

The first tension is very clear in *Brighton Rock.* As stated in that novel, it is the contrast between the world of good and evil on the one hand and of right and wrong on the other. Pinkie and Rose live in the world of good and evil. They know the struggle men are engaged in transcends the outward, the visible and the moral; they know eternal life is at stake. Ida Arnold, the friendly, extrovert tart, who pursues Pinkie to avenge the murder of Fred, her acquaintance for a brief while, knows all about right and wrong, but nothing about heaven and hell or good and evil. For that reason Rose dismisses Ida herself contemptuously as nothing.

The same conviction that the sphere of good and evil somehow transcends the level at which people speak of right and wrong appears in the other novels. Sarah's holiness in *The End of the Affair* cannot be evaluated in terms of right and wrong. Her previous sexual promiscuity and her deep adulterous love of Maurice Bendrix were stages of the emergence and growth of her holiness, despite its final moral demands. The drive to holiness she experienced was no mere desire for moral rectitude.

The second tension appears most strongly in *The Heart of the Matter,* though it runs through the other three. It is the tension between Catholicism as an objective system and the complex reality of human experience and existence. Graham Greene treats the Catholic sacraments, the Catholic moral code, and the objects of Catholic belief, such as heaven and hell, as forming a spiritual universe, understood by Catholics as more real and more important than the visible universe. The Catholic spiritual universe has its laws. Certain kinds of action have certain kinds of consequences. The Catholic knows all the answers. He knows how the system works, what to do and what not to do in the spiritual order in which a man's salvation or damnation is decided. The novels, particularly *The Heart of the Matter,* take the Catholic system as the frame of reference for the principal characters and then deal with the dilemmas arising from its failure to fit the situation or correspond with the promptings of the human heart. The reality of the system is not questioned, but its inadequacy creates conflict.

I do not think that Greene has handled the two religious themes I have mentioned very successfully. His theological insight does not match his literary skill, with the result that his religious situations and dilemmas are artificial and unconvincing. Nevertheless, his discernment of a double tension in the Catholic religious outlook—I should myself say in every religious outlook—is penetrating and fundamentally sound.

Religion is the drive toward transcendence, the thrust of man out of and beyond himself, out of and beyond the limited order under which he lives, in an attempt to open himself to the totality of existence and reach unlimited reality and ultimate value. This drive cannot be confined to the observance of a moral code settling questions of right and wrong within a limited frame of reference. The person who is merely moral knows nothing of the heights and depths of human experience and existence.

Even a religious system set up to mediate the drive toward transcendence cannot contain it. It never fits exactly and at its best is inadequate precisely because it is in itself limited and relative, not transcendent and absolute.

In brief, the drive toward transcendence is in tension with both morality and external religion.

To make this concrete, however, we have to consider the function of religion in society and consequently in relation to moral codes.

The social order is the environment necessary for life at the human level. The human world, the world in which a man must live in order to be human, is the world created by society and culture. Men are not born into a world ready-made for them by nature. Even the biologically necessary activities of eating and sex do not operate as self-sufficient instincts in no need of education; they must be formed and guided by society.

The different social worlds are humanly constructed—products of social collaboration. Consequently, as a human construction and open to change, each and every social order is inherently precarious. Its maintenance demands the sustaining of a particular pattern of thought and behavior against the destructive force of individual and group interests and initiatives, and against the disintegrating impact of other cultures. To achieve that and give its particular world stability a society creates a system of legitimation, through which are transmitted reasons and explanations justifying its ideas, laws, and institutions, and showing them to be right.

At this point we meet religion in one of its most constant functions. The religion of a society is its comprehensive scheme of meaning. It provides the universal framework within which particular social institutions, convictions, values, and practices find their meaning and which gives them their ultimate justification. It overarches society, in the phrase Peter Berger chose as the title for his book, as a sacred canopy.

The legitimating function assigned to religion as the ultimate foundation for the social order explains why religion appears in history predominantly as a conservative influence. For it to be on the side of law and order corresponds to one of its original functions. Men rightly dread the collapse of the meaningful pattern that gives order to their human existence. They have traditionally looked to religion to provide a deep and secure foundation for the pattern they regard as true and real. In short, a function of religion is to support the established order.

The history of society from preliterate cultures through the great civilizations to the emergence of modern society with the French Revolution shows religion functioning as a bulwark of the existing social structure. Traditional or premodern societies were organized as integrated religio-political systems.[1] They shared the following characteristics. The ideological component was provided entirely by religion, so that religious ideas maintained the legitimacy of the system and specifically of the ruler. Again, the political community was identified with the religious community in theory and substantially so in fact, so that religious dissent equaled political disloyalty. Further, it was religion, not an efficient governmental apparatus, which enabled the ruler to maintain stability in the realm over considerable periods of time. Finally, religious specialists confirmed the ruling power by rituals and inculcated obedience in the people, while the ruler on his part exercised extensive religious functions. In brief, religion gave meaning and legitimacy to society and served as a powerful means of social control.

Religion in traditional societies was taken for granted as part of the social order rather than felt as oppressively conservative. Tension, however, arose whenever society was undergoing change and the established order was being brought into question. Religious authorities in such a situation have often mistakenly aligned themselves with the rich and powerful, who resist change because of their vested interests in the existing setup.

Such support for the established order against change is peculiarly out of place in modern society. This, as we saw earlier, is not built upon religious principles. Whatever its disadvantages in other respects, it should at least leave religion freer to exercise its prophetic role of denouncing social injustice and taking the side of the poor and weak. What in fact has for the most part happened in modern society is that the conservative function of religion, originally a benefit to the whole of society, has been corrupted into a support of wealth and power out of institutional self-interest. In the struggle to survive and prosper in the modern world, institutional religion has come to terms with the Establishment.

Leaving aside notorious instances, such as Pius XI's support of Mussolini's imperialist adventure in Ethiopia or the segregationist practices of the churches in the South of the United States, I will take two quieter examples to show how religion has continued to exercise a conservative role in modern society.

Some readers may know the trilogy, *Lark Rise to Candleford,* by Flora Thompson, which has become a minor classic of English literature. With vivid and intimate truthfulness and irresistible charm, the three autobiographical volumes preserve a picture of rural life in England in the 1870s and 1880s. There, without any polemical emphasis, we are told how religion functioned to keep the lower orders in their place during a period of social change. This is from her description of the preaching of Mr. Ellison, the Anglican rector:

Another favourite subject was the supreme rightness of the social order as it then existed. God, in His infinite wisdom, had appointed a place for every man, woman, and child on this earth and it was their bounded duty to remain contentedly in their niches. . . . Less frequently, he would preach eternal punishment for sin, and touch, more lightly, upon the bliss reserved for those who worked hard, were contented with their lot, and showed proper respect to their superiors.[2]

My second example is from present-day America. Garry Wills, in *Bare Ruined Choirs,* describes the bewilderment of the FBI agents—mostly Catholics—at having to track down and arrest priests like Daniel Berrigan, who were resisting the State in the name of Christ:

Little in the agents' personal experience, he writes, equipped them to answer such hard questions. They were brought up to consider all Authority as one, in church and state, and to think of priests as especially allied with American values against all "outside" forces (for outside, read Communist). How, then, cope with a force not only inside the country and its citizenry, but deep inside the Catholic structure of holy things?[3]

In other words, American Catholicism, never officially part of the social structure of America, has in great measure become a conservative force, upholding the Establishment and its version of law and order.

Mention of Daniel Berrigan brings us, however, to the other side of religion. Genuine religion, religion not denatured, is and always has been a dangerous force for any society to invoke.

While religion supports the social order by providing a comprehensive scheme of meaning, it tends to weaken the hold of that order upon its members by denying its ultimacy. Although the transcendent side of religion has often been kept severely in check by established interests, religious movements have again and again proved disruptive of the existing social order. Only with much qualification can religion be historically described as a conservative force.

To put it in this way: religion relativizes the order it consolidates. But note that the relativism inculcated by religion differs from the relativism of the skeptic. The skeptic uses the limited, incomplete nature of all formulated truths and values to restrict the human drive toward truth and value, and to cast unresolvable doubt upon any claim to an experience of ultimate truth and value. For religion the relativity of any human order of truth and value indicates its mediatory function. Its purpose is to become transparent, to lead beyond itself and mediate a transcendent experience.

The two apparently contradictory functions of religion, consolidation and transcendence, come together in the single function of mediation. Men are led to self-transcendence, but only in and through a particular institutional order.

Seen as a system of mediation, religion established a threefold institutional order. The three elements are an organized set of rites, an ethical code and legal system, and a body of doctrine. Rites, ethics, doctrines—the three may be brought under the general heading of religious action. In the Hindu tradition they constitute the *karma mārga*—the way of action or the discipline of deed. In Hinduism the *karma mārga* is complemented by the *bhakti mārga,* or the way of devotion, and *jnana mārga,* or the way of insight or contemplation. To bring ritual actions, ethical codes, and doctrinal orthodoxies under one heading helps us to grasp the mediatory function of institutional religion, a function it exercises through these three connected elements. The link with the other two elements illuminates the role of each. Further, the grouping of all three under the category of action or good works immediately warns the religiously perceptive against taking the correct observance of any or all of the three as sufficient for genuine religion without faith or devotion or religious insight.

The religious term "sin," it may be noted, has had a range of use corresponding to the grouping I have made. Although the sense of ethical wrong has now become almost exclusive, we cannot understand religious history without recognizing that "sin" has also meant faults against ritual correctness or doctrinal orthodoxy. To remember that may prevent us from identifying ethical fault with sin in the deeper sense of a lack of religious spirit or love, whether that expresses itself in ethical, ritual, or doctrinal deviation or in a correct but empty performance.

It is in the context of religion as a system of mediation that we may best view the problem of moral absolutes, so troubling to religious people today in our so-called permissive society.

Mediation, I have just said, brings together the two functions of religion: one, the consolidation of a particular social order; and, two, the drive toward transcendence. It is the drive toward transcendence that originates and grounds absolute moral values, such as justice, love, mercy, generosity, chastity, compassion, and so on. These values denote the goal of the human drive toward transcendence; they designate the ultimate, unlimited reality toward which men strive in pursuing value. The absolute moral values are so many names of God.

When these names are used of finite instances, so that we speak of justice, love, and the rest as instantiated on earth among men, they continue to refer to absolute values. The actions of men are of absolute value insofar as they are actions of men open to transcendent reality and acting under the impetus of their drive toward ultimate value. Justice in concrete instances means the actions of just men, and just men are those who are dynamically open to the God of justice whether they name him or not. Just as all the names of God refer to one and the same reality, so, too, all the absolute moral values are one and indivisible. The different virtues and values roughly classify different manifestations of the same attitude toward the one, ultimate reality, different expressions of the thrust toward ultimate value.

Just or loving actions, then, are the actions of just or loving men as just or loving and have an absolute value. They unconditionally demand our approval; they are morally good in an unconditional way. At the same time, such actions cannot be precisely classified and catalogued nor brought under a set of moral rules—for two reasons.

First, because they spring from creative freedom. The thrust of men toward the ultimate in a movement of self-transcendence is the source of their creativity in making themselves and their world. We may formulate men's past achievement in past situations, but not their future possibilities in new situations.

Second, because all concrete instances of justice, love, and the rest embody absolute value in representative and symbolic fashion as not confined to them but transcendent. To claim a set of moral rules as themselves absolute and an adequate formulation of justice and other values is an idolatry parallel to taking our images and concepts of God as adequate representations and formulations of the divine nature.

Not the drive toward transcendence, but the other function of religion, namely, the consolidation of a particular social order, originates moral codes, just as it originates rites and doctrinal orthodoxies.

I would stress the importance in human living of that consolidating function. Men cannot live without the imposition of some social, institutional order upon the flux of their experience. Nevertheless, all such orders and their components are relative. In themselves they cannot claim an absolute value or a universal necessity.

To speak of a particular order as relative does not mean that it is the product of individual or group caprice. A good social order will be the result of creative intelligence and freedom, and designed both to increase the quality of human living and to release and foster the drive toward transcendence. But none of this makes the order with its prescriptions an unchanging absolute.

This brings me to one of the most persistent and perhaps deadliest of the temptations of religion, the temptation I am calling the anger of morality.

By this I mean the insistence upon an established pattern of behavior and thought for its own sake, so that it loses its mediatory quality and becomes a closed order as an end in itself. I call it anger, because psychologically the attitude I am describing would seem to be a hostile reaction that chokes love, a bitter rejection of what is free and does not conform, the sharp repulsion of anything that disturbs or threatens an enclosed self.

Since the established pattern that may be angrily insisted upon is threefold, namely, ritual, ethical, and doctrinal, we find three similar forms of distortion. These are familiar to us as ritualism (in a pejorative sense), legalism, and dogmatism. All three manifest the same fundamental failing, that is, a restrictive insistence upon a particular institutional order, so that instead of facilitating the movement of men toward self-transcendence, it becomes a rigid framework that imprisons them. Here, however, I want to direct my attention to the working of this temptation in the area of moral values and conduct. Hence I have called it the anger of morality. But there should be no difficulty in applying my remarks to the other two areas.

The anger of morality is more than the periodic inertia that defends an obsolete system and resists change. An underlying factor is the human fear of freedom, of love, and of self-transcendence. That fear can turn with hatred as well as anger upon those who manifest an openness one is afraid to allow oneself. It is the personal repression of self-transcendence that leads people to seize upon an institutional order as an instrument for suppressing the feared drive in others. Law and order becomes the cry of the repressed against the free.

Rosemary Haughton, in her book *Love,* shows in some detail how the organization of human life so often suppresses love, a word she uses in the sense of the self-giving form of the drive for self-transcendence. In writing of child-rearing, which after all is the process of socialization and thus shows the working of the social order, she says: "In fact the study of child care, both in the past and present, is largely a study of the restriction or suppression of love."[4] Men fear the openness, the self-transcendence, the self-giving of love, and this fear often cripples the mediatory function of their institutions and of the code of behavior these demand.

The anger of morality is a temptation for every social order and institutions, even those making no explicit appeal to religion. It appears as the failure to recognize the inadequacy of any particular institutional order in relation to reality and human experience as a whole. Man is taken as made for the law, instead of the law as being made for man. Any movement that cannot be contained within the established order is feared and suppressed.

But distinctively religious institutions are subject to more virulent forms of the temptation. Because of their direct concern with the transcendent absolute when they turn in upon themselves, lose their openness and mediatory capacity and become closed institutions, they fall into a self-idolatry and claim an absolute value for themselves. They do so in effect if not in words. The consolidating function of the religious system in sustaining a stable, meaningful order is no longer complemented by its function of promoting the human drive beyond every limited order to reality and truth as transcendent. Why? Because the religious system cannot bear to be itself surpassed and relativized. Hence the order ceases to mediate and becomes so much dead weight.

The manifest example today among religious institutions of yielding to the anger of morality is the Roman Catholic Church. Its insistence upon its traditions as absolute is destroying its capacity to mediate the human drive toward transcendent value insofar as this is creative of new patterns of moral behavior, new forms of social order, new types of institutions. The manner in which the Roman Church handled the question of contraception did more than result in a wrong decision; it was a sign of a deep-seated corruption, which placed the relative value of an institution above the absolute value of genuine morality. The drive toward transcendence is indeed powerful within the Roman Catholic Church and the potential of that church for the renewal of human life is immense. But Roman Catholics are struggling in the tenacious grip of an organized system closed in upon itself, unable to mediate because it cannot bear to see cherished traditions, laws, and institutions left aside as obsolete.

Though in terms of a particular historical situation and debate, St. Paul expresses what I have been saying in his contrast between a life according to the Spirit and a life according to law.

For Paul life according to the Spirit implies freedom from the yoke of external law. He tells the Galatians: "If you are led by the Spirit, no law can touch you";[5] and he speaks to the Corinthians of the new covenant, "which is not a covenant of written letters but of the Spirit; the written letters bring death, but the Spirit gives life."[6]

These texts and others like them are not adequately interpreted by referring to the overelaborate prescriptions of the Jewish law. St. Paul is contrasting two different ways of living: a life consisting in the careful observance of an institutional order with its rites and laws, and a life that moves through and beyond externals in the freedom of the Spirit. The scrupulous carrying out of a series of laws is not yet a life in the Spirit. It is sub-Christian. Life according to law is a crude form of morality. External law has a preliminary, educative, mediatory function. According to Paul, law had this educative function in the history of Israel, which until Christ was under the tutelage of the law. Law has a similar function in the life of every individual. Without the mediation of law, men might well confuse the demands of the Spirit with the fantasies of self-indulgence. It is because we do not love, because our feeble love is not to be trusted, that we have to be brought under the discipline of law and have imposed upon us from without what should come freely from within. But all law is inadequate and crude. It cannot cover the complexities of human existence. It does not and cannot express the delicate sensitivity of love in the innumerable situations of daily life. Could a loving husband and wife in a set of laws codify the demands love makes upon them in their life together? No more can we codify the demands of the Spirit of love in our movement toward God.

But, above all, law is not the source of Christian living, which does not consist in the observance by men of a law from God. The Christian life is the inpouring of God's Spirit into our hearts to open them to the self-transcendence and self-giving of love. All laws and institutions are but means. They are therefore relative and changeable.

Our so-called permissive society is a society in a state of transition. It is not permissive because of a lesser adherence to moral values, nor, on the other hand, because people are fundamentally more tolerant of social deviance. The permissiveness reflects an uncertainty how to embody moral values in the concrete when the old forms no longer fit and the new have not yet clearly emerged. When a new social order, whatever its value, has established itself, conformity will once more replace permissiveness.

In this situation Christian churches other than the Roman Catholic have their share of the anger of morality. Despite many writings and utterances with appropriate, forward-looking sentiments, the average congregation remains enclosed within a narrow moral code, unable to see the inadequacy of its morality or to regard any departure from it as other than sin. Many Christians are refusing the drive toward transcendent value because in our present situation it urges them on beyond the familiar, the comfortable, the safe.

The churches encourage their refusal, because for all the fine words they are afraid of moral nakedness. They will not strip themselves of their traditional clothing in a creative movement toward a more suitable garb. Living religion and morality today cannot be codified in a stable fashion, because this would demand integration into the existing social order, an order which has proved itself a moral failure.

The problem of appealing to any moral code in our present society is illustrated by the debate on abortion. I have found people whose moral sensitivity I respect in perplexity over this issue, because every position seems to violate some moral values. I myself find it difficult to rest in any conclusion, though my predominant feeling is against abortion.

The absolute stand of the Roman Catholic Church against abortion has only hardened the opposite refusal to admit any restriction upon women in the disposal of the fetus. Both sides are hiding behind supposed absolutes and are failing to acknowledge the complexity of the problem. Further, the Church's case has an unconvincing ring because the insistence upon this single moral norm is not accompanied by sufficient evidence of sensitivity to the relevant values. To repeat what has often been said: the Church does not show the same concern about the taking of innocent lives in war or by economic exploitation. Moreover, its saving-of-face decision on birth control, its attitude to illegitimacy, its lack of concern for poverty, bad housing and other social injustices: none of this sits happily with moral indignation about abortion. On the other hand, I find it difficult to have much respect for either the moral sensitivity or the arguments of those who advocate unrestricted abortion. Admittedly, the legal question is distinct from the moral question, although the distinction is being ignored by those promoting abortion as much as by those condemning it. At the same time, granted that to regard abortion—at least in some instances —as morally wrong is not the same as saying it should be legally prohibited; moral values are part of the legislator's concern.

What, then, in practice? Insistence upon the laws of a moral code is, I suggest, the wrong approach to abortion as in general to the moral problems of this period of transition. Nor do I think that any law as a rule of behavior can be defended as absolute for reasons I have already stated. The chief requirement when the demands of morality are unclear is a careful attempt to disentangle all the values at stake. Next should come an identification of the social obstacles blocking the recognition or attainment of any of those values. Efforts can then be made by those sensitive to particular values to change the social institutions and conditions that threaten them. With abortion, as with any other serious moral issue, what in the last analysis is in question is the kind of social order we want and are prepared to work for in practice, and the most important distinction between one social order and another is in the transcendent values each embodies and mediates. While we work to change society in a defective area, practical moral and legal decisions in that area are bound to have something of an interim quality, in which one preserves as many values as possible in a situation allowing only ambiguous decisions. A self-transcending openness to values rather than a closed insistence upon moral laws is what counts in a time of transition from one social order to another.

But I want to offset any impression that the refusal to make a moral code absolute always implies doing less than the code demands. It may often mean doing more. Moral values, I am contending, transcend their embodiment in a particular social order with its institutions and laws. A creative openness to values will therefore confront people with imperatives beyond any at present codified. The anger of morality is not overcome by moral laxity, but by moral creativity.

Recently reading Herman Melville's story *Bartleby,* I was struck by the way it illustrated that point. Melville in his great adventure story, *Moby Dick,* depicted the modern Promethean in Captain Ahab. But Ahab, driven forward to confront the hostile reality of an evil universe with fierce defiance, is perhaps more a nineteenth-century figure than a contemporary man. With *Bartleby,* first published in the 1850s, we have an astonishing anticipation of a twentieth-century image of man. In reading *Bartleby,* the inescapable comparison is with the stories of Franz Kafka.

To show its relevance to our present theme necessitates some elaboration and commentary.

The narrator of the story is a lawyer in chambers in Wall Street, New York, which look upon a white wall at one end and a black wall at the other. He is the employer of three clerks, and upon being made Master in Chancery advertised for another copyist, or scrivener. In answer to his advertisement came the young man Bartleby, a figure "pallidly neat, pitiably respectable, incurably forlorn." The lawyer engaged him.

To have him at immediate call, he placed Bartleby on his own side of the folding-doors dividing his office, putting him behind a high green screen. At first Bartleby copied industriously, working day and night, but writing "silently, palely, mechanically." Then not long after Bartleby's arrival, his employer asked him to help in checking the accuracy of a copy. He was stunned "when, without moving from his privacy, Bartleby, in a singularly mild, firm voice replied, 'I would prefer not to.' " A repetition of the request brought the same answer, "I would prefer not to."

His composure disarms his employer. The latter as narrator comments: "Not a wrinkle of agitation rippled him. Had there been the least uneasiness, anger, impatience or impertinence in his manner; in other words, had there been anything ordinarily human about him, doubtless I should have violently dismissed him from the premises. But as it was, I should have as soon thought of turning my pale plaster-of-paris bust of Cicero out of doors. I stood gazing at him awhile, as he went on with his own writing, and then reseated myself at my desk."

Other calls, quite usual for a lawyer's clerk, are made upon him, but each time he quietly and mildly replies, "I would prefer not to."

The baffled employer begins to observe Bartleby more closely. The scrivener never went to dinner, but seemed to live on the small cakes called ginger-nuts. He was in the office before anyone else arrived in the morning and remained behind in the evening after the others had left. Happening to call into his chambers one Sunday, the lawyer found Bartleby there, and it became clear to him that Bartleby made his home there. The thought of the poor clerk's loneliness filled him with "a feeling of over-powering stinging melancholy." But when afterwards he asks Bartleby about himself, the clerk tells him he prefers not to answer his questions.

The employer again challenges Bartleby on his behavior in refusing ordinary demands and asks him to begin to be a little reasonable. "'At present I would prefer not to be a little reasonable' was his mildly cadaverous reply."

Despite his usual industry in copying, Bartleby was seen to fall into standing reveries at his desk. The time came when it was noticed that he did nothing but stand in his dead-wall reverie. He told his concerned employer that he had given up copying.

He remained as a fixture in the office. At last the lawyer dismissed him. But Bartleby did not go, and when told he must replied, "I would prefer not."

Unable to get rid of Bartleby, the lawyer moved his chambers. Bartleby remained in the old chambers and when turned out of the office remained in the building on the stairs and in the entry. The new tenant, holding the lawyer responsible for Bartleby, comes to him and insists that he do something. He tries to persuade Bartleby to go, even offering to take him home with him until he finds some suitable arrangement. To no avail. Bartleby replies, "At present I would prefer not to make any change at all."

The lawyer rushes out and flees his office for several days to avoid being hunted out by the new tenant. He returns to find that Bartleby has been removed, and that he is requested to go and tell the authorities what he knows about Bartleby. He goes and, after seeing the officer, asks to have an interview with Bartleby.

"And so I found him there, standing all alone in the quietest of the yards, his face towards a high wall, while all around from the narrow slits of the jail windows, I thought I saw peering out upon him the eyes of murderers and thieves.

" 'Bartleby!'

" 'I know you' he said, without looking round—'and I want nothing to say to you!' "

When the lawyer points out that the prison "is not so sad a place as one might think," Bartleby replies, " 'I know where I am.' "

When the lawyer goes a second time and is led to Bartleby, apparently asleep, huddled at the base of the wall of the yard, he discovers that the poor scrivener is dead.

As with every profound work of literature, there is more than one reading of *Bartleby*. Melville has created an image that remains long in the imagination, provoking fresh thoughts and emotions.

We can see Bartleby, the scrivener, representing contemporary man: forlorn, lonely, miserably friendless, isolated from society and his fellow men, on the margins of human existence, an exile lost in a foreign world. He is finally overcome by this world of death. The prison is appropriately named "The Tombs." Its Egyptian style of architecture, with the walls of amazing thickness, reminds the lawyer of the pyramids. When the lawyer on discovering Bartleby dead is asked if the man is asleep, he murmurs in reply, " 'with kings and counselors' "—a quotation from the Book of Job, from the passage where Job curses the day of his birth and wishes he had died from the womb and thus been at rest with kings and counselors of the earth who build tombs for themselves. " 'Ah Bartleby! Ah humanity!' " is the exclamation with which the story ends.

Does Bartleby contend like Job? He does not explicitly protest his lot as Job did. Even less does he meet the hostile universe with violent defiance as does Captain Ahab. But he does present a passive resistance that preserves him as a self, though on the very edge of personal existence. " 'I would prefer not to.' 'You *will* not?' urges the employer. 'I *prefer* not' gently insists Bartleby."

The drama of the story lies in the relationship between Bartleby and his employer. The lawyer is not just the narrator but a protagonist.

He presents himself as a man who makes no great demands upon himself or others. From his youth he "has been filled with a profound conviction that the easiest way of life is the best." He adapts himself to the idiosyncrasies of his employees. He is moved to sympathy for Bartleby. He tries to help him. He tolerates him far beyond the point that society in general would consider reasonable. His other employees show themselves much more intolerant toward the recalcitrant clerk.

Nevertheless, Bartleby, I suggest, presented the lawyer with a demand that he had not so far recognized and that in the end he failed to meet, namely, a demand for the simple unconditional acceptance of another as a person. "I prefer not to" is not only a softening of "I will not" into a more passive less active resistance, but also includes, I think, an element of request, of address to the other; it is a plea for acceptance of the stated preference. Bartleby is presenting himself with his own unusual, unprecedented attitudes and needs to his employer.

At first glance the employer would seem to have fulfilled all the requirements of charity. He offers him money for his sustenance, he allows him to make the office his home and indeed offers to bring him to his own house, he is concerned when he thinks Bartleby is sick, and finally he visits him in prison. Besides, then, fulfilling all the requirements of justice that any worldly court would have demanded of him, he would seem to have fulfilled the demands of love as set forth in the account of the Last Judgment in Matthew 25.

Yet he does not truly accept Bartleby. Even at a superficial level his motives for concern are mixed: "Yes. Here I can cheaply purchase a delicious self-approval. To befriend Bartleby; to humour him in his strange wilfulness will cost me little or nothing, while I lay up in my soul what will eventually prove a sweet morsel for my conscience." At a deeper level, when he resolves to get rid of Bartleby, he too easily dismisses the possibility of reaching him spiritually: "I might give alms to his body; but his body did not pain him; it was his soul that suffered, and his soul I could not reach." Ironically, as narrator the lawyer tells how he overcame a wave of murderous resentment against Bartleby "by recalling the divine injuction: 'A new commandment give I unto you that ye love one another,' " and he goes on to remark how charity operates as a prudent principle, a great safeguard to its possessor. Gradually the very limited charity of the lawyer breaks down. He becomes ashamed of Bartleby before his professional colleagues who visit his office on business. He cannot bring himself to thrust him, "the poor, pale, passive mortal," out of his door, but he abandons him to the new tenant: "the man you allude to is nothing to me." He knows that society could not charge him with any failure of responsibility. His own conscience frees him—but not quite: "I now strove to be entirely care-free and quiescent; and my conscience justified me in the attempt; though, indeed, it was not so successful as I could have wished." The truth is that he had failed to respond to what was indeed a most unexpected and unreasonable but a clear and personal demand for transcendent love.

There are many Bartlebys today: out of joint with society, unable to operate and communicate within it. The demands of morality are not fulfilled by those who plead they have done everything and more than the law requires, if they have failed to meet the uncodified—indeed uncodifiable—implications of being open in love to another person coming uninvited into their lives.

To conclude: there are open people and closed people, open institutions and closed institutions.

Open people are those who are open to truth and love. They are ready to go beyond themselves. They are not afraid of reality even when it leads them beyond all limits into the ultimate. They are not afraid of love. They are able to love and trust others, and they do not refuse faith, which is a loving trust of ultimate reality. Open institutions are those which serve to mediate such openness and do not confine human experience within the limited order they create.

Closed people are those who refuse to go beyond themselves. They cannot bear much reality and call a halt to seeking for truth as soon as the drive for truth draws them on beyond the familiar, the comfortable, the safe. They are afraid of losing themselves in a self-transcending, self-giving love, whether human or divine. Closed institutions minister to the fears of such people by suppressing any movement that cannot be contained with the order they establish.

The search for a perfect institutional order of morality is illusory, because any institutional order of its nature is limited and exists to be surpassed. But institutions serve an indispensable mediatory function, provided they resist the temptation angrily to impose their morality as an end in itself.

The churches have less excuse but a greater temptation than most to do so. Their ineffectiveness is the measure of the degree to which they have succumbed to the anger of morality.

NOTES

1. Donald Eugene Smith, *Religion and Political Development,* The Little Brown Series in Comparative Politics (Boston: Little Brown, 1970).

2. Flora Thompson, *Lark Rise to Candleford,* The World's Classics (London: Oxford University Press, 1957), pp. 229–30.

3. Garry Wills, *Bare Ruined Choirs: Doubt, Prophecy, and Radical Religion* (Garden City, N. Y.: Doubleday, 1972), p. 235.

4. Rosemary Haughton, *Love* (Harmondsworth: Penguin, 1971), p. 4.

5. Galatians 5:18 (Jerusalem Bible).

6. 2 Corinthians 3:6 (Jerusalem Bible).